A STUDY OF RACES
IN THE
ANCIENT NEAR EAST

A STUDY OF RACES
IN THE
ANCIENT NEAR EAST

BY

WILLIAM H. WORRELL
Associate Professor of Semitics, University of Michigan

CAMBRIDGE
W. HEFFER & SONS LTD.
1927

First Published in 1927

PRINTED IN ENGLAND

To the memory
of my Mother

Preface

THIS study has grown out of lectures which were first given at the summer session of the Jewish Institute of Religion, New York City, in 1921, and later at Columbia University and the University of Michigan. They would never have been written without the encouragement of Dr. Stephen S. Wise, nor published without the benevolent interest of the late Dr. Israel Abrahams. In a way they have sprung from a life-long romantic interest in race, which has been fed and deepened by long contact with the Jewish people of many lands. They are The Race.

As I stand before these faces, representing many types, I fancy I see in real presence Hittite and Babylonian, Canaanite and Aramaean: now all "Jews," many American citizens, some eminent in modern life, speaking the Germanic-Romance language of the British Isles, or the medieval German of the Rhineland, or the Spagnoli and Arabic of Moorish Spain. Once, I know, their forebears wrote works in Arabic, and before that in Hellenistic Greek and Aramaic, and before that in Hebrew. They came out of Arabia, the fountain-head of Semitic speech. Behind the intricacies and mysteries of Arabic lie the revelations of ancient Akkadian and Ethiopic. But this is only the beginning: The pictured monuments of Egypt tell us that the most archaic Semitic speech is no more than an early offshoot of a trunk whose branches even now flourish all over Africa. With this type of speech there went a race which by degrees we trace back to the Atlas highlands. We fancy we can almost follow them across into Europe, and imagine them the builders of Stonehenge and the dolmens of Brittany. Perhaps they were the people of Druidism. It may be that Caesar's soldiers heard in

Aquitania the last echoes of European Hamitic speech; and that Goidels and Brythons learned from Pictish mothers the idioms of this pre-Aryan British tongue. And may not this have been, indeed, the language of the whole Mediterranean race?

It became a personal necessity, and seemed not a useless labour, to collect the material which came in my way and bore upon this racial and linguistic story, interweaving with it my own unpublished notes and studies of a more original and exact nature: not indeed in the pompous manner of a scientific monograph, bristling with footnotes and references, and obscured by digressions and discussions of priority: but in a simple manner, agreeable to general readers, and not offensive to the learned. The only difficulty lay in making of one literary texture such a combination of popular exposition and occasional technical discussion. I should perhaps have distinguished typographically this difference in the material. But, after all, my readers—who, I hope, will be of many sorts—may choose and skip according to their tastes and interests, and without offence. It was, of course, necessary in certain places to give philological material in support of other-wise daring statements; but I hope that even this will be found interesting to many readers of linguistic tastes, although they may not be orientalists.

In the course of such study other material came to hand; and it seemed possible to build up a sort of system in which the Hamitic-Semitic chapter could be placed so as to harmonise with tenable views about other races of Europe and the ancient Near East. For this I can claim no great originality.

Lastly: To be of much use to the general reader the study had to include some brief discussion of geographical setting and of the historically most important peoples of the Old Testament, without attempting to say any-thing new.

PREFACE

It is a great pleasure here to express my indebtedness to my colleague, Professor A. E. R. Boak, for reading the manuscript and making a number of corrections and suggestions; to my colleagues Mr. Robert B. Hall and Mr. Otto E. Guthe, for the two maps; to Mr. G. A. Wainright, of the Department of Antiquities, Cairo, for two photographs of objects in the Egyptian Museum and for permission to publish these; to Vester and Company, of Jerusalem, for permission to use a number of their very unusual photographs of oriental human types; and, lastly to Anne MacKenzie Worrell, for revision, proof-reading and the index, as well as much helpful criticism.

W. H. WORRELL.

ANN ARBOR,
January, 1927.

Contents

List of Illustrations

Although race, culture, and language are distinct, their course for long periods is often parallel. Racial admixture is reflected in the phonology as in the syntax of languages. When one member of a speech-family suffers loss of characteristic sounds or sound-distinctions, that may well be a sign of alien admixture, and even an index of the degree of admixture.

True, racial mixture often falls behind linguistic blending; for a community may be led or forced to change its type of speech abruptly, and there may exist at the same time barriers to intermarriage, as in the case of the American Negro. He has, up to the present, acquired only a little of the white man's blood, and, on the other hand, a great deal of the white man's language. In time Negro English will disappear, and in time also the Negro. In the end all will have the Negro strain, and the speech of all will show it. After Time has established equilibrium, language may become a true index of race.

CHAPTER I.

Geography

THE ancient Near East includes ordinarily: (1) Palestine (with Syria and the Syrian Desert); (2) Egypt (with Sinai); (3) Babylonia (with Assyria); (4) Asia Minor (with Armenia); (5) Arabia (with South Arabia); and (6) Persia. India, though intimately related to Persia and Islam, belongs to the Far East; and Greece, in spite of the Greeks of Asia Minor, belongs to the West along with Italy. The ancient Near East includes then the lands of the Old Testament narrative and of those religious traditions which touch the life of the world through Judaism, Christianity, and Islam.

EARLY QUATERNARY GEOGRAPHY

In early Quaternary times the Sahara was a well-watered region of great fertility and abundant life, a refuge for the men of Europe when driven southward by the ice. North-western Africa was connected with Europe and the British Isles. White men passed across the land-bridges, back and forth, in their struggles with changing climate and with each other, in Neolithic times attaining a certain type of culture and speech. The rest of Africa was occupied by men of the Black, and Asia by men of the Yellow race.

In spite of the complexities of modern ethnology there remain three fundamental varieties of mankind: White, Yellow and Black; and these varieties centre in the three continental areas of the Old World: Europe, Asia and Africa. Here they must have been specialised during long periods of separation. All past and present races of men appear to have resulted from mixtures of

1

THE ANCIENT NEAR EAST

these fundamental varieties, in different ways and in varying degrees. The process began very early, and has become infinitely complex.

While more recent writers[1] assure us, beyond any reasonable doubt, that the Sahara was a part, in fact, the chief part, of the Eurafrican breeding ground, older writers[2] held that in early Quaternary times northwestern Africa was separated from the rest of the continent by a Saharan sea. The first view is based upon abundant evidence, geological, zoological, historical, and philological. The second view seeks to account for the presence of certain marine shells in the Sahara, and was doubtless encouraged by its utility as explaining the separateness of Eurafrica from Africa of the Blacks.

ANCIENT GEOGRAPHY

Before the beginnings of history the continents had assumed nearly their present shape and interrelation. White men had gone across Asia into Polynesia. Yellow men had entered the North Polar region and the Western Hemisphere, and mixed with the Whites in Malaysia. White men of one group had penetrated Africa to the Cape, and had taken possession of Arabia. Other White men formed a nucleus in the steppes of eastern Europe, and Yellow men a similar centre on the plains of western Asia. From these three steppe-lands came repeated streams of migration, pouring into more fertile regions. The "Fertile Crescent," extending from southern Palestine to the Armenian mountains, and back to the head of the Persian Gulf, is a region very often entered by migrations from Arabia, eastern Europe and western Asia.

ANCIENT CLIMATE

Comparison of modern conditions in the Near East with ancient conditions, as revealed by historical

[1] Keane, *Man, Past and Present*, 2nd edn. (by Quiggin and Haddon), 1920, pp. 445 ff.
[2] Brinton, *Races and Peoples*, 1901, pp. 88 ff.

sources, seems to point to a great climatic change. This part of the world appears to have dried up. Where there once were communities well endowed with material wealth and conscious of the claims of higher culture, there are now only backward populations completely taken up with the struggle for existence. Everywhere is dryness and delapidation. Huntington[3] calls attention to the old Roman bridges which now span waterless gullies in Syria; to the evidences of the use of wooden beams in northern Syria, now without timber; to the numerous spring-houses, baths, and works of hydraulic engineering that now lie high and dry in the desert. Gerasa (Jerash) cannot at present support enough people to fill the seats of one of its ancient amphitheatres. Nearby are the ruins of three water-mills, two large public baths, and a reservoir for naval sham battles, with the remains of the aqueduct which brought the water. Palmyra, which was able in the third century A.D. to extend its dominion over Syria, Mesopotamia, and part of Egypt, is now inhabited by about fifty miserable Arab families which with difficulty exist upon its scanty sulphurous and brackish waters. Petra, centre of great caravan routes at about the same period, is now without a single inhabitant or drop of water. Its routes, to Gaza, the Gulf of Akaba, and the Persian Gulf, have all been deserted. In the sixth century B.C. large numbers of Jewish men, women and children twice made the journey between Jerusalem and Babylon, presumably straight across the Syrian Desert; and among the woes they suffered thirst is never mentioned. Nowadays all caravans must make the long detour by way of Palmyra or Aleppo. The Sinai Desert once supported the Children of Israel for a considerable time, but now it can be traversed only with difficulty. According to the census of David, in 2 Samuel xxiv. 9, there were then ten times as many people in Palestine as at present, and therefore a much greater food supply.

---

[3] *Palestine and its Transformation*, London, 1911, p. 288.

As the fertility of the soil is unquestioned, there must have been a greater supply of rain. The oasis of Khārja, west of the Nile, is now, according to Hobbs,[4] only about one per cent. fertile, and yet bears evidence of an ancient stream and water-fall near which grew an oak tree.

It is therefore impossible to believe that the Near East has always been as dry as at present. It is true that with the decay of antique civilisation the accumulated equipment of mankind in this part of the world was allowed to fall into disrepair, and this has made matters worse. But that will not account for the great change itself. For some unknown reason there are great cycles of variation in temperature and humidity in certain places. The American South-West is one of these, and the Near East another. Deforestation does not decrease rainfall, although trees store up moisture and lengthen the moist season beyond a critical point. There has been actually less rainfall in the Near East, for the Dead Sea and the Caspian are much lower now than they once were.

Within historical times, however, the Near East has never been moist according to our ideas. It always has had a Mediterranean climate. Palestine has always been a land of cisterns. The age of oak trees in Egypt must have been extremely remote. Huntington thinks that a change of not more than two or three degrees of temperature has occurred. It was a little colder, and the rainy season was therefore a little longer; and there was more snow to lie upon the ground and saturate it.

PERIODICAL CHANGES

Not only has the Near East been more moist than at present, but it has before been just as dry as at present, and even drier. Hobbs noted this fact in Upper Egypt. Huntington found that the Jordan strands

---

[4] *Geological Review*, iii. 5, May, 1917; *Annals of the Association of American Geographers*, vii. 25 ff.

indicate dry periods at about 300, 600, 1200, and 1800
A.D., following a 300-year cycle, but omitting 900 and
1500. Besides this cycle of 300 years, others of three,
eleven, and thirty-five or thirty-six have been suggested.

CAUSE OF MIGRATION

It has been observed in present-day Palestine that
the nomadic border Arab tribes do not attack the
settled population wantonly, but only when there is
drought and consequent failure of pasturage. The
struggle for existence among people of the steppes is a
struggle for water and pasturage. When these decrease,
or when the population increases, which amounts to the
same thing, economic pressure compels movements of
population in the direction of the most ready relief.
Since the population steadily increases, and the moisture
recurrently diminishes, there are both continuous and
intermittent migrations from the steppes and deserts
into the fertile land. Huntington describes the
migration of an Arab tribe from north-western Arabia
to Tunis, in the early seventh century, A.D. They were
driven out of their haunts by drought; and, once in
motion, kept going until their impetus was spent, or
until they found a place whose population they were
strong enough to dislodge. It is significant that this
occurred just before the great outpouring of Arabs
which accompanied the expansion of Islam. In fact
the irruption of Arabs from the Arabian peninsula,
though set in motion by the religion of the Prophet,
was the result of a long process of gradual desiccation,
for which there is no lack of evidence. There is every
reason to believe that the other great migrations of
Semites from Arabia, at approximately 3500 (Babylonian), 2500 (Canaanitish), and 1500 (Aramaean), B.C.,
were caused by periodic recurrence of drought; and
that the Aryans left the steppes of Russia, and the
Turanians the steppes of central Asia, for the same
reason. The great migrations which took place

everywhere after 375 A.D. must have been caused by the arrival of a critical point in a progressive drying up of these great breeding places.

Present Climate

The lands of the Old Testament lie within the region of winter rains. But not all of them have a dry summer and a wet winter. Upper Egypt has no rain at any time of year, because its prevailing winds come from across the Libyan desert. Alexandria has frequent rain in winter, because its winds come from across the sea. Cairo has one or two showers, in mid-winter. In Palestine and Syria there is abundant rain from October till May, especially on the western slopes and highlands, because here there are open coasts, exposed to winds that have swept the length of the Mediterranean. The rest of the year is dry. As one goes northward the rainy season lengthens; but the great land masses of Asia Minor, Armenia, and Persia, become so heated that these countries have a dry summer like Palestine. Arabia receives a little rain, mostly on the narrow western coastal plain, because its westerly winds are moistened a little by passing over the Red Sea.

Africa and Asia

Geologically Africa includes that part of Asia which we now call Mesopotamia, Palestine and Syria. It meets Asia along the frontier formed by the Persian Gulf and the mountain-walls of Persia, Kurdistan and Asia Minor. Arabia and the Syrian Desert are merely the extension of the great deserts of northern Africa, which consist of horizontal strata, broken only by occasional mountain ranges and depressions due to geological faults. Persia, Armenia, and Asia Minor, on the other hand, like central Asia, consist of deeply folded mountains whose valleys have gradually become filled with their debris.

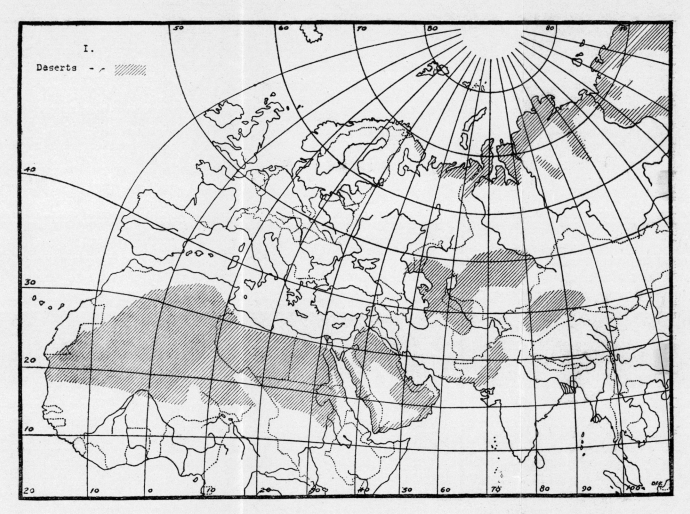

Drawn by Mr. Otto E. Guthe upon the outline map of Mr. Robert B. Hall, both of the Department of Geography, University of Michigan, according to W. Köppen, *Die Klimata der Erde*, 1923, pp. 121-2.

The Fertile Crescent

Palestine, Syria and the valleys of the Tigris and Euphrates form a sort of "Fertile Crescent"[5] about the Syrian Desert, which is a limestone plateau, scantily and briefly covered with grass in its northern part by the winter rains. In a way the history of the Near East is a struggle between the people of the mountains and the people of the desert for the possession of the Fertile Crescent. The population, which slowly expands by natural increase, and periodically migrates because of drought, in the steppe-lands of Arabia, Russia, and western Asia, is drawn to this region of greater fertility. Aryan emigrants from Russia and Turanian emigrants from Asia came in through Persia. Semitic emigrants from Arabia entered either from the eastern end or the western end of the Crescent. In doing so they probably followed the "wādis," or gullies, which, when they do not contain water, offer the best prospect of securing it by digging beneath the surface. The most conspicuous of these are the Wādi ar-Rumma, which begins in the western part of Najd, and ends near the confluence of the Tigris and Euphrates, at the head of the Persian Gulf; and the Wādi Sirhān, which extends from the Jauf into the Haurān district of the East Jordan country. Both of these are still used for caravan routes from the great central highland of Najd, the true home of all Northern Semites.

Egypt

In remote times the waters of Lake Victoria Nyanza, seeking lower levels, found a tortuous path along the Libyan plateau northward, and emptied at last into the Mediterranean at a point near ancient Memphis or modern Cairo. It wore its bed deeper and deeper, reaching sea level as far up-stream as the Second Cataract, in Nubia. The valley of this river, the Nile, was a peculiarly happy place for human habitation.

[5] A convenient term of recent and uncertain origin.

It presented a long narrow strip of very fertile land,
continually enriched by alluvial soil, and copiously
watered from the unfailing sources of the Abyssinian
highlands. Being practically rainless, it enjoyed sun-
shine all the year round. The same river afforded
ready means of communication from one end of the
country to the other. On both sides it was guarded
by deserts. Here there came into being a race, of
Hamitic origin, remotely and intimately mixed with
another element which we cannot doubt was Negro.
Like all Hamitic peoples around the eastern "horn"
of Africa, they were a variety distinct from the Libyan
or Berber type of north-western Africa. This was
Egypt proper, and these were Egyptians in the oldest
sense of the term.

The Delta

In the course of time the Nile had built up a delta[6]
like that of the Tigris and Euphrates and the Mississippi.
From the point near Memphis, where the river had
poured from a notch of the plateau, into the sea, the
river-silt formed a low-lying swampy country, traversed
by a network of sluggish streams. This may still have
been its condition in the time of Menes (c. 3300 B.C.);
but it was inhabited by Libyans, superior to the people
of the valley. Egyptian civilisation resulted from the
fruitful union of "Upper Egypt," the valley, and
"Lower Egypt," the Delta.

The Egyptian religion presents an aspect of hetero-
geneous, undigested conceptions. In some cases two or
three distinct strains are discernable. This may
indicate different racial elements in the people.

Egyptian Climate

Egypt is intolerant of foreign plants and animals.
The common deciduous trees and the European races,
do not flourish there. Northern races suffer most;

___
[6] First used of the Nile Delta.

but it is a question whether even the Greeks can maintain themselves, except perhaps in Alexandria, on the coast. One sees no indication nowadays of any Greek strain in the peasantry; although the papyri indicate that the Greek language was in general use from about 300 B.C. to 300 A.D. throughout Egypt.

Oases

A chain of remarkable oases is found in the Libyan desert, west of the valley of the Nile, and roughly parallel to it. As Hobbs[4] has shown, they are caused by the action of wind-blown sand upon a geological fault. The deeper, water-bearing strata are thus exposed, or brought within the reach of boring operations, which seem to have been practiced from early times. The most famous are Sīwa and Khārja, both of which lie upon the caravan route which leads toward the west, and are historically a part of Egypt.

Somewhat different is the large depression to the west of the Nile, not far south of Cairo, which is watered by an overflow of the river that reaches it by a narrow channel through the desert. It is called in Arabic al-Fayyūm (Egyptian: Pi-Yōm, "The Sea") because of the important lake in its centre. Within historical times the lake has grown steadily smaller; and the ancient island of the crocodile cult, Soknopaiou Nesos, now lies some two and a quarter miles inland, buried in desert sands. The Fayyūm has yielded a great quantity of Greek papyri. In the Coptic period it cultivated for a time its own dialect of that language.

In the Libyan Desert, west of the Delta, lies the Natron Valley, famous in the history of monasticism. It is a region of salty lakes, the remains perhaps of an ancient arm of the sea.

Libya and Nubia

Although there were caravan routes via the oases, Egypt was never entered by invaders except from the

northern or southern end of the valley of the Nile. In
the north the Libyan tribesmen filtered into the army
as mercenaries; and reached the throne in the Twenty-
Second Dynasty.

Its greatest danger in the south was the Cushitic-
Hamitic people who centre in the "horn" of eastern
Africa. The Twenty-Fifth Dynasty was "Ethiopian,"
probably of this stock from which the valley Egyptians
themselves were derived.

SINAI

From the north through Sinai came also Asiatic
invaders; sometimes from Palestine and Syria, by the
route along the shore of the Mediterranean; and sometimes from Arabia, probably by the route that joins the
head of the Gulf of Akaba with the head of the Gulf
of Suez. The former communicates with the western
end of the Fertile Crescent, and so also with northern
Arabia. The latter passes along the coastal plain of
the Hejāz into South Arabia.

The Sinaitic peninsula is a desert, rising in mountains
toward the south. Here the Egyptians discovered and
mined copper, so necessary to their arts and crafts.
Somewhere in this region is the holy mountain, connected with the primitive cult of Yahweh and the
Mosaic dispensation. There are several fertile and
well-watered wādis which afford facilities for the resting
of caravans and the transfer of goods. A considerable
number of Hebrews traversed Sinai in the course of
their slow migration from the Nile Delta to Palestine,
and must therefore have found sustenance. The
peninsula has never been the seat of any civilisation.

ARABIA

Arabia is a land of great importance to the history
of the Near East and of the world, although that importance is indirect. It does not possess the economic
resources necessary ever to have made it the actual

seat of great imperial power. But it is the breeding
ground of virile peoples who established political power
in adjoining lands; and it produced the ideas and the
organisation which made the Islamic world.

Very little is known of the history of Arabia, or even
of its present condition; although it is larger than India,
and lies midway between Europe, Asia and Africa,
surrounded by the great trade routes of ancient and
modern times. The reason for this is its peculiar in-
accessibility. Its northern desert, the Nefūd, is difficult
for Europeans to traverse; its southern desert, the
Ruba' al-Khāli, is hardly accessible even to Arabs.

Its Dryness

Arabia has no rivers, and hardly any rainfall; and
yet it supports a vigorous and prolific population.
The effect of its rigorous conditions of life is to produce,
by natural selection, a race whose powers of endurance
are unequalled even by those of Iranian and Turanian
nomads, who are bred by similar conditions. The
basis of this selection is the extreme dryness of the
Arabian peninsula. Its prevailing west winds bring
some moisture to the coastal plain along the Red Sea,
and even to the top of the plateau. Oman, in the east,
also has some rain. But still Arabia is one of the driest
countries in the world. How then is any human life
possible?

Oases

An examination of Hogarth's map[7] shows a large
number of widely scattered fertile spots, or oases, and
extensive fertile tracts. The oases, in conjunction with
the wādis or gullies, in the bottoms of which water
can always be found by digging, make possible the
great caravan routes. Arabia is one great limestone
plateau, tilted up on its south-west, along the Red Sea
coast, and sloping therefore toward the north-east.

[7] *The Penetration of Arabia*, 1905.

The waters beneath it apparently do not issue forth until they have reached the eastern coast.

ROUTES

Of the many routes through the peninsula, the most important are: 1. From Basra in Transjordania to Hā'il in Najd by way of the Jauf. It connected the western end of the Fertile Crescent with the centre of North Arabian culture. 2. From Damascus in Syria to San'a in Yemen by way of Medinah and Mecca. It connected the western end of the Fertile Crescent with the centre of South Arabian culture. 3. From Basra in Mesopotamia to San'a in Yemen by way of Boreida in Najd (and Mecca?). It connected the eastern end of the Fertile Crescent with both the North Arabian and the South Arabian cultural centres. The first and third of these follow in part the great wādis, Sirhān and ar-Rumma, and probably are the routes mainly pursued by the great Semitic migrations into the Fertile Crescent. The second of them is the trade-route between India and the West along which came the reports of fabulous wealth in South Arabia. It has been the main highway of Arabia since the appearance of Islam.

Migration occurred by another path also. Perhaps at about the beginning of the Christian era the present Semitic population of Abyssinia crossed over to Africa from South Arabia by way of the straits of Bab al-Mandeb.

YEMEN AND NAJD

The land of greatest fertility or moisture lies in the south (Yemen) of the peninsula. It has produced and sustained civilisations for long periods. Probably all the Semitic languages which have the so-called "broken plurals" (Arabic, South Arabian and Abyssinian groups) were developed here. Less fertile or moist was the central highland (Najd).   It is the rallying point of the North-Semitic nomads.   Probably all the Semitic languages which lack the broken plurals (Akkadian, Canaanitish, and Aramaic groups) were developed here. After the Aramaean migration (c. 1500 B.C.) Najd seems to have become occupied by people who spoke the type of Semitic native to the south, because then no more Semitic languages of the old Northern type came out of Arabia.

It is necessary to suppose that the Semites in Arabia were divided into two communities for a very long period; and that North-Semitic languages, which do not have the broken plural, sprang from a different ancestor than the South-Semitic languages, in which the broken plural is an essential feature.   The most probable places for these two communities are Najd and Yemen.

RACIAL PURITY

Arabia is so uninviting a place, compared with neighbouring lands, that it has never suffered much invasion.   Its population, on the contrary, as we have seen, has constantly flowed outward from it.   One might fairly assume, therefore, that the Arabs are a pure or homogeneous race.   This would be far more true of the Arabs of Najd than the people of the Hejāz, Yemen and Hadhramaut, and Oman, who came more in contact with the outside world because they occupied the borders of the peninsula.   The Hejāz is traversed by a great highway of trade.   Oman is in contact with India and Persia.   Yemen and Hadhramaut stand in very close relation to the adjacent Cushitic lands of Africa and their people show a physical relationship to the Semitic-Hamitic peoples of Abyssinia.   There was a great deal of passing back and forth.   The Semitic blood in Abyssinia came originally from some part of South Arabia, and the Abyssinians later returned to that country as colonists.

INVADERS

Esarhaddon, king of Assyria (B.C. 681–668), relates that Sennacherib (704–681), his father, had conquered "Adumu, a fortification of Aribi," and that he increased the tribute which they had to pay. In the third year of his reign, with the help of the kings of Aribi, he penetrated to the land of Magan.[8] "Aribi" refers to a people in the north-west of Arabia, and is not improbably identical with "Arab." "Magan" refers to a remote part of Arabia, and strongly suggests "Ma'an" an ancient kingdom in Yemen. The terrible Assyrian, who usually "climbed difficult mountains like a wild ox," was so subdued by the fearful privations of his march through Arabia that he saw "two-headed serpents" and animals that "flapped their wings." His Assyrian god revived the remnant of his drooping army, and he returned to Assyria in a manner which he does not chronicle.

Caesar Augustus in the year B.C. 24 sent the Roman general and Praefect of Egypt, Aelius Gallus, into South Arabia with orders to effect relations with "Arabia Felix" by treaty or conquest. It was supposed to be a land of great wealth because it supplied Rome with articles of luxury, such as frankincense, cassia, myrrh, topaz, and pearls. These articles, of course, though of great value when brought in small quantities to Rome, were of little value in the land of their origin, and in any case could not be eaten nor drunk. Strabo,[9] a friend of the general, gives an account of the desert terrors, heat, thirst, disease, and treachery of "Happy Arabia." It lacked even the meagre necessities of a hardened Roman soldier. It was invincible because of its incredible poverty, wildness, guile, and treachery. He took a number of miserable towns with his ten

---

[8] Prism A, Col. II, III; K. 3082, S. 2027: following Winckler, *Keilinschriftliches Textbuch zum Alten Testament*, 1903, pp. 50, 53; Schrader (Zimmern-Winckler), *Die Keilinschriften und das Alte Testament*, 3rd edn., pp. 89–90.

[9] xvi. 780 f.

thousand men; but he could not take Ma'rib, his first
fortified city, because his men had no water to drink;
so he retired with great losses, in disorder and disgust.
The Abyssinians, from the second to the sixth
century, succeeded in taking and holding parts of
South Arabia. The Turks, though good soldiers and
themselves Muslims, were never able to assert effectively their authority beyond a few garrisons.

SETTLED LIFE

Arabia is not entirely a land of nomads. Wherever
there is enough moisture the year round to support a
settled population, there agriculture is practised and
towns grow up. The business of the towns is trade
and the accommodation of caravans. The latter
includes the exaction of tolls and considerations for
"protection," which often means merely immunity
from further molestation.

Southern Arabia is more moist and fertile than any
other part, and therefore developed considerable civilisation. The beginnings of it are known only through
references in the cuneiform literature. For the Hebrews
Ma'ān, Saba, and Hadhramaut were remote places of
fabulous wealth: "The kings of Sheba and Seba shall
offer gifts," "And to him shall be given of the gold of
Sheba," "And they shall sell them to the men of Sheba,
to a nation far off."[10] South Arabia was known to the
Judaeans only through its commercial outposts and
representatives in north-west Arabia, and the articles
of luxury brought north along the Hejāz trade-route.
Much of the merchandise came from India; and when,
in the first two centuries of our era, the trade of India
was diverted to the Red Sea route, South Arabian
prosperity vanished, its irrigation works fell into decay,
and its people migrated northward, in some cases
becoming nomads. A great many South-Arabian
inscriptions have been found and deciphered; but,

[10] Psalm lxxii. 10, 15; Joel iii. 8.

C

unfortunately, they tell us little of the character or chronology of that interesting civilisation.

The caravan stations along the trade route through the Hejāz did not share much in the culture of South Arabia. The settlements in Najd must have existed in very early times, but nothing came of them. In the period just before Islam shepherds scratched their trivial and ribald *graffiti* in a South Arabian character as they wandered among the black lava blocks of the Syrian Desert. The old pagan poetry that has come down to us in Arabic tells us very little of the life of the northern Arabs before Islam.

THE SYRIAN DESERT

The Syrian Desert is a continuation of the Nefūd, and therefore a part of Arabia rather than of Syria. It has always been occupied by nomadic (bedawi) Arabs, from Najd or even from Yemen. On its borders is the Fertile Crescent. At ordinary times the nomads wander about in search of pasturage, and contend among themselves for the possession of their ranges and wells, raiding each other and the border as occasion permits. As the population increases, a period of drought, or severe snow storms, will move them to attack the settled (hadari) people of the border. Thus individuals or groups settle down, at first tentatively, then permanently, along the border lands, as they may be observed to be doing at present in southern Palestine. The shores of the Fertile Crescent are repeatedly and continually washed by waves of bedawi migration. At times they have been inundated.

None of the great powers that have occupied the borders of the Syrian Desert have been able to defend them effectively against the nomads, except by enlisting for a time the aid of some border tribe.

SYRIA AND PALESTINE

In its most ancient sense, "Syria" (Suri) meant all

Photograph by]   *[Vester & Company, Jerusalem.*

ARAB TENTS

the lands "between the two rivers" Tigris and Euphrates, from the borders of Babylonia in the south to the mountains of Armenia and Anatolia in the north. These lands were at about 1500 b.c. overrun by Aramaic-speaking Semitic nomads, who at first gave it their name, "Aram," but later were called, after its name, "Syrians." The northern part was comparatively fertile, but "Mesopotamia" was of little value.

Later the term "Syria" was applied to "Coelo-Syria," the rich valley between the two Lebanons, and then to the western slopes of the Lebanon, the old Phoenicia. Finally these lands came to usurp the name entirely.

Syria is sometimes made to include its southern extension, Palestine. Together they form the western end of the Fertile Crescent. Palestine is small and rocky. Syria has good land, though not very extensive, along the coast and in the valley. In the north it runs off into steppes.

Taking "Syria" in its later sense, and including Palestine for the present, one may say of the whole that its outstanding feature is its broken surface. It is geologically young: East of the Jordan are lava-fields, and near the Dead Sea are sulphur deposits. Although the bee-line distances are small, in practice it is difficult to get about in the country. North and south runs the Great Cleft. It begins, in the north, as Coelo-Syria, continues, after an interruption, as the Jordan valley, and becomes finally, in the south, the shallow Wādi Araba and the deep Gulf of Akaba. The average height of the Lebanon is over 6000 feet, and Mount Hermon rises to 9383 feet, above sea level. The Jordan valley for most of its course is below sea level, and reaches at least a depth of 1392 feet at the Dead Sea. The western side of the Great Cleft (al-Ghor) rises to some 3000 feet, and then descends by terraces to the sea. The eastern side, Transjordania, begins more abruptly at about the same height, and is continued as the Syrian Desert. Syria proper has two rivers, the

Orontes and Leontes, which empty into the sea, but are unnavigable. The streams of the Antilebanon all discharge into inland lakes and lose their waters by evaporation. In Palestine the only river of any size is the Jordan, which flows through the Great Cleft to the Dead Sea. The other so-called rivers hardly deserve the name, as they are little better than wādis, filled at one time with tumbling waters, and at other times quite empty. None of them facilitate communication and transportation. Everywhere the country is cut and seamed with ridges and gullies.

Syria has a number of natural harbours, the most important in ancient times being the Phoenician cities of Tyre and Sidon, and in modern times, Beirout. Palestine has only Jaffa, a very poor place to land, in any weather, because of its rocky and tempestuous approach. Haifa seems to have been of little importance, probably because of its shallowness.

Syria is much more fertile and well watered than Palestine. The western slopes of the Lebanon, the valley of Coelo-Syrian, except toward the north where it runs off into steppes, the beautiful Damascene oasis on the edge of the Syrian Desert, fed by the icy waters of the Barada : Palestine has nothing to compare with these. Of the Holy Land, the coastal plain is nowhere very wide, and always subject to invasions of sand from the sea. The Plain of Esdraelon is now rather swampy. The best part is still the Haurān in Transjordania, and the region around Samaria. A great deal of Palestine consists of limestone hills, covered with grass and wild flowers in the spring time, but otherwise unproductive and unattractive. The trees have disappeared, and the soil has slipped down into the valleys. The abundant rains of winter hasten down the wādis to the sea and the Jordan.

In prehistoric times Palestine was visited or inhabited by a people who built dolmens, cromlechs, and menhirs, like those which are found in the British Isles and France, and along the northern coast of Africa. Palestine was probably influenced by the "cultural drift," if not actually by the blood, of those remote wanderers and traders whom we connect with the Hamites, and Iberians, and the oldest stratum of people in the British Isles. At about 2500 Semitic immigrants came from Arabia, and settled in the lowlands, where they became known as Canaanites or "Lowlanders." Their brethren who settled on the coast from Carmel northward became the Phoenicians, and other related groups, the Moabites and Ammonites. "Amorite" may have been a general term applied to them all. The Semitic immigration of about 1500 B.C. brought the Aramaeans or Syrians into Coelo-Syria, and the Israelites into Palestine. At about the same time the Philistines, fleeing from Crete, took possession of the southern coast, as far north as Jaffa, or even Dor. A comparatively feeble Semitic migration of about 500 B.C. brought Nabataeans into Edom, and pushed its old population up into southern Palestine. It is useless to try to enumerate the possible sources of racial admixture in Palestine, for it has always been a land of turmoil. Hittites, Kuthites, Babylonians, Persians, Greeks, Arabs, Mongols, Franks; all of these have doubtless left their mark upon the population.

BABYLONIA AND ASSYRIA

The Tigris and Euphrates rise in the highlands of Armenia and Kurdistan, flow in a south-easterly direction until they mingle in the Shatt al-Arab, and empty at last into the Persian Gulf. Near ancient Babylon, or modern Bagdad, the two rivers approach one another, thus forming two large areas: an upper, Mesopotamia, and a lower, Babylonia. East of the Tigris in its upper courses lay Assyria. These three areas combined form a great part of the Fertile Crescent, though Mesopotamia and Assyria are far from fruitful now. In earliest Babylonian times the two rivers emptied separately into the Persian Gulf at the ancient city of Eridu. As the site of this city is now far inland, and as there are no old Babylonian settlements below it, we must conclude that the rivers have greatly altered their courses, and that the Gulf has receded as the alluvial plain at their mouth has advanced. The whole of Babylonia indeed is an alluvial plain, the product of the Tigris and Euphrates, just as the Delta is the gift of the Nile. Like the Delta, Babylonia was crossed and re-crossed by a network of streamlets. These were in antiquity supplemented by canals which distributed the water so as to make a very large region habitable, in spite of the floods of springtime, and the drought of the rest of the year. The canals are now all but obliterated, and the land is now either desert, steppe, or swamp.

Sumer and Akkad

In earliest times Babylonia was called Shinar, and was divided into two parts: a southern, Sumer, and a northern, Akkad. Mesopotamia proper was "Syria" (Suri), as we have seen. From Greek times onward the name "Mesopotamia" has been applied to all the region "between the Rivers."

Persia

Persia is, next to Arabia, the largest of Near-Eastern countries. It is part of the great south-west Asiatic plateau, made up of deeply-folded mountain ranges, whose valleys have become filled with debris. Along its northern border and in its west-central portion lie mountain chains over 10,000 feet high. None of it is well watered except the northern slope of the Elburz range. Most of the population at present is to be found in the north-west and west. The eastern desert is inhabited by nomads. The central part is so extremely dry as to be uninhabitable. Persia has a long, dry summer, and not very much rain even in winter and

early spring. Its besetting evil and great selective
natural force is drought. In its manner of life it resembles Arabia and the Syrian Desert, although its
people belong to a different human family.

In its present condition at least, Persia is not a land
to attract migrations. When, at different times, Aryan
or Turanian hordes moved into it from the north-east,
they could hardly have been attracted by fertility or
moisture superior to that of the northern steppes. They
must have been set in motion by drought and over-
population, and so moved onward without purpose.
In this respect they differed from the Semitic nomads
who from time to time invaded the Fertile Crescent
from Arabia; for here there must always have been the
report of better conditions in a land "flowing with milk
and honey." It was always through Persia that
Aryans and Turanians came to the Fertile Crescent:
sometimes the one, sometimes the other, and sometimes
the two joined in loose confederation.

Armenia

Armenia lies to the north-west of Persia and is a
part of the same highland region. Its surface is very
irregular, and broken by mountains and depressions.
Ararat, some 17,000 feet above sea level, is one of the
highest peaks in western Asia. The depressions are
from one to two thousand feet below the general level,
and are occupied by lakes, such as Van, Urmia and
Gokcha. About the lakes the soil is fertile and watered
by mountain streams, but in the highlands agriculture
is impossible, and life becomes nomadic. The difficulty
of communications is in striking contrast to Egypt and
Babylonia, or even Arabia and Persia, and the population tends to remain or become diverse rather than
homogeneous.

To the north of Armenia stands the impenetrable
wall of the Caucasus mountains. The Aryan nomads,
who were bred in the adjacent part of southern Russia,

were therefore effectively cut off from the south by the Black Sea, the Caucasus, and the Caspian Sea. When they entered Persia, it was by a route east of the Caspian; and when they entered Asia Minor and Armenia, it must have been by a route west of the Black Sea. The modern Armenians probably got their physical appearance from the ancient "Alpine" race, earliest inhabitants of this region, and their language from Aryans who came in through Asia Minor.

ASIA MINOR

Asia Minor (Anatolia) is similar in formation to Persia and Armenia, but not so high nor so broken. It is a table-land, with mountain ranges on the north and south, a low coastal plain, and long valleys running east and west. The western coast alone is deeply indented and full of harbours, from which lines of travel extend up the valleys to the highlands. The low coast plain naturally attracted seafaring people. Those who settled on the west coast could easily approach the central plateau by following the valleys. Approach was also easy from the direction of Armenia. But Asia Minor was well protected from disturbances arising in the Fertile Crescent or lands still further southward, by the Taurus range. Islam was brought to it by the Turks, from a partly Arabised Persia, and not by the Arabs themselves. The Hittites of history represent an "Alpine" white race, closely allied to the same element in the Armenians, and either autochthonous or derived from Armenia, organized into a political confederacy by Aryans who came in along the valleys from the west of Asia Minor.

At the present time the central part of Asia Minor is dry, and much of it is given over to nomadic life.

CHAPTER II.

Ethnology

OLD TESTAMENT

DOWN to the Persian period the only lands at all well known to the writers of the Old Testament were the Delta and the valley of the Nile as far as Assuan, Sinai, and the Fertile Crescent. Lands and peoples beyond these limits were mentioned, but they were afar off and little known. Within this familiar region the most important peoples were Semitic and Hamitic.

In the oldest Biblical reference to ethnology, the blessing and curse of Genesis ix. 25–27, written probably in the second millennium B.C., there are only three peoples: (1) Shem, or the supposed descendants of a man of that name, meaning Israel. (2) Canaan, or the old inhabitants of Syria and Palestine. (3) Japheth, or invading northern people.[11] The three are " brethren," in the sense that they are all of the human family. The Israelites have conquered, or hope to conquer, the Canaanites; and they regard the northern people as friends. In the prose passage (ix. 18) in which these verses were incorporated we are told that Canaan is the son of Ham, and that Shem, Ham and Japheth are sons of Noah. There may have been much more folk-lore information in the mind of these old writers; but the scheme as it stands really accounts for only Israel, its enemies, and its friends.

About the seventh or eighth century B.C. the account in Genesis x. was written, from which the modern terms "Semitic" (through the Latin of the Vulgate) and "Hamitic" are taken. In general it places Aryans

---

[11] Gunkel, *Genesis*, 1902, pp. 71 ff.

to the north and Hamites to the south of Israel, which is quite correct. It must have been, however, upon some primitive comparative philology, for Joktan, Hazarmaveth (Hadhramaut), and Sheba are rightly assigned to the Semitic group, people related to Israel, although they lived in extreme southern Arabia. Political relations and national prejudice play some part; for Canaan, Nimrod (Assyria), and Mizraim (Egypt), national enemies, are all made the children of Ham, although the Canaanites and Assyrians were Semitic. Also there is some contradiction, for Assyria (Asshur) and Sheba appear both as Hamitic and Semitic. The most striking defect is the lazy metonomy by which names of peoples, countries, cities, and imaginary ancestors are used indiscriminately. Nations are supposed to consist of tribes and families which are descended from one ultimate common ancestor. These ancestors can be placed in a family tree at the head of which is Adam, "Man." It is a habit still among Arabs to regard adopted and allied people as blood brethren. But we know that neither mankind nor any group of men descended from an individiual. Finally, this genealogy covers the Near East only, and takes no account of the vast areas of the world beyond, at that time certainly inhabited.

CLASSIFICATION OF RACES

No satisfactory basis for the classification of races has yet been found. The difficulty lies in the fact that groups of men are related to one another in three ways: in body, culture, and language; and that classification in one way does not necessarily coincide with classification in the others.

LANGUAGE

Language is an almost inseparable part of culture, and both of these tend to be retained and handed down in a group of people who are physically related; but the group may change its manner of living and its speech without a *corresponding* physical change, as the Negroes in the United States have done, or the Jews throughout the world. A group may migrate into another cultural and linguistic area, or be invaded by people of alien speech and culture, or be influenced through less intimate contact, especially by a superior culture or an enterprising religious propaganda. Of the early distinct human varieties which we assume, none are to be found even at the dawn of history. Man is already very old. His repeated migrations over vast distances are no longer to be traced. All communities, wherever found, consist of people thrown together in one place, blended by association and selectively shaped by environment. The people need not be of one origin. Frequently they are as varied as the people of the United States. But if left alone for a sufficient time the racial strains are blended into a uniform type, and culture and speech become one, distinct and authoritative.

On the other hand in the long run a change in culture and speech does entail some change in blood. It is believed by many that there are few if any Negroes in the United States without White admixture, in spite of laws forbidding inter-marriage, and the most pronounced and effective social pressure upon all who attempt social intercourse. The Whites do not yet associate with Negroes, but they become parents of "Negro" children. In the course of time the Negro, who now is Anglo-American in speech and culture, will be more and more Anglo-American in blood. The Jews throughout the world partake strikingly of the characteristics of their Gentile neighbours. This is due partly to the local manner of life, and to the unconscious selection of mates in accordance with Gentile standards of beauty and desirability; but there must be a great deal of mixture of blood, especially in times of distress and disorder. Physical assimilation lags far behind cultural and linguistic assimilation; but it is always in progress.

Genesis x. 5, 20, 31, mentions language as one of the distinguishing marks of peoples, and the story of the Tower of Babel, in Genesis xi., goes further and supposes that the original reason for racial divisions was a sudden confusion of tongues: quite in contradiction of the theory of descent from separate ancestors, to be found in Genesis x. For primitive and naïve people speech undoubtedly is the most noticeable difference between "us" and "them," because it is the most effective bridge or barrier to social intercourse. Greeks could get nothing out of their "Barbarian" neighbours but "bar-bar-bar," and the Arabs had a similar experience with the "Berbers" of Libya.

Unless the resemblance is very great it may escape notice entirely. A Dutch peasant would probably observe familiar features in German, but certainly not in French or Russian. Individuals of one Aryan group are not aware of kinship with another. The Semitic tongues happen to be very closely related—almost as closely as the different Romance languages—but the writers of Genesis x., for instance, were not in a position to compare the languages of the Near East outside the Semitic group. Often speculation is guided by dogmatic considerations, as when it is supposed that Hebrew was the original language of mankind. Or it is superficial and unmethodical, as when "obey" is derived from Hebrew "Obed," "Potomac" from Greek "potamos," or "chauffeur" from Hebrew "shofar." Such antiquarian speculation brought down upon itself much well-deserved criticism. At length it was learned that languages may be safely compared only by employing a definite method and by postulating certain laws. Vocabulary may not be compared without reference to principles of sound change. Morphological or structural resemblances are far more important than vocabulary. Franz Bopp in the middle of the nineteenth century founded the comparative grammar of the Aryan languages. His studies appealed to the popular imagination of a wide circle of "Aryans," and gave rise to erroneous notions about language, especially the confusion of language with culture and race. But they led to better comparative study of the Semitic languages, which had its roots back in the seventeenth century, and of the Turanian and other groups.

CULTURE

What has been said of language also holds of culture and civilisation, for language is only one of the social institutions, and a part of the *mores*. But even here a distinction can be made. It is possible for people to use certain weapons or eat a certain staple food and yet be of different speech. The use of bronze or iron spread regardless of tongue or race. The Japanese share the Chinese culture, but have an entirely unrelated language. This influence has been appropriately called "cultural drift."

RACE

What we really mean, when we ask for the racial relationship of a group, is its physical relationship. Even when we are discussing language or culture we have this idea in the back of our minds. It is the thing we are most interested in : either because we think that "blood will tell," or because we feel an enormously enlarged family pride, or weakness for genealogies.

The first stage in physical ethnology is the observation of general resemblances. It is quite easy to have intuitive impressions about people, and very difficult even for trained ethnologists to say just what the reasons are for their judgments. Polynesians are said to possess White blood because of their regularity of feature, and probably the impression is correct ; but this is far from being the exact thing which a botanist does when he dissects a flower or plant and assigns it to its place in his system. It is very much like describing and relating different kinds of dogs; and for much the same reason, for the races of men are, like the breeds of dogs, only varieties of one great species.

A race should be defined in terms of physical characteristics. Among the many physical characteristics of individuals, certain ones should be chosen as conveniently distinguishing groups from one another. But which ones shall be chosen, and how many shall be taken at once, has not yet been decided. The problem is to make such groups as can be arranged in a system which is not self-contradictory nor historically inconceivable. There appear indeed to be three fundamental varieties of mankind, White, Yellow and Black, and this coloration of the skin refuses to be permanently affected now by climate, whatever climate may have had to do with it in some former age of great variability. The White has mostly wavy hair, the Yellow straight hair, and the Black woolly hair; but there are exceptions in each case, unless we shift our ground and begin to invoke other considerations. The White race includes both short-headed and long-headed strains, which would otherwise be very conveniently assigned to the Yellow and Black, respectively. The tallest of men are probably the Hima in East Africa; but the next tallest are found in Scotland or among the Scandinavians of Minnesota. It is plain that no classification can be made upon the basis of one characteristic; and yet no two sets of characteristics can be made perfectly parallel. In the end then one must retain the categories, White, Yellow and Black, and understand them to include other than skin-colour characteristics.

The fact is that the observable varieties of mankind are too closely related to furnish the distinguishing characteristics of species. Whatever distinct varieties there may once have been, we now have only admixtures and mixtures. There was a long and complex history of which we know nothing. We cannot even be assured that only three original varieties are involved. There may have been intermediate or undifferentiated ones. The Bushmen of South Africa have extremely fine woolly hair, so sparse that it appears to grow in "pepper-corns"; but they are more yellow than black. Have they anything at all to do with the true Negro? The Dravidians of India are almost black, but they have abundant wavy hair; the Papuans are very black, but they have abundant woolly hair on both head and face, and convex noses. Are these specialised forms, or mixtures, or independently evolved races of black skin?

Anthropological Account of Man

Study of existing glaciers led to recognition of glacial remains in places where these ice rivers cannot now maintain themselves because of the low latitude and altitude. In former times glaciers extended much nearer the equator than at present. At those times the Northern Hemisphere at least, and perhaps the Southern Hemisphere, were much colder. Such living things as were able to move, and were not cut off by the seas, must have migrated toward the equator; the rest either perished or adapted themselves to the new conditions. The ice advanced and retreated four times. In the warmer periods man must have enjoyed easier conditions of life and more leisure for activities not absolutely requisite to survival. In the colder periods he must have developed stamina, intelligence, and resourceful-ness in the struggle for life. The sea was not always at its present height. When it advanced his com-munications were cut off, and he became specialised by in-breeding, and by peculiar habits of life and social ideals which affected mating. When it receded he undertook great migrations, and mingled his blood with that of peoples whom he met on the way, and with whom he settled. Thus there came about strongly marked varieties, and also innumerable kinds and degrees of mixture. Perhaps we can discern, beneath the crossing and re-crossing, a variety of man associated even to this day chiefly with each of the great Old World continental areas. It may well be that in some part of Europe there developed a race with less deeply coloured skin, hair and eyes; in Asia another race, with darker skin, uniformly black and perfectly straight hair, dark eyes, and a peculiar formation of the eye-lids; and in Africa (with some relation to Melanesia?) a third race, with extremely dark skin, and black woolly hair. All other races may conceivably be derived from these. Perhaps the Melanesians are a branch of the same race as the African Black, the Polynesians derived distantly from the White, the Amerinds (American Indians) distantly from the Yellow, and the Malays from a remote amalgamation of the White and Yellow.

The ultimate origin of man lies far back of the time of his specialisations and migrations. On the whole it appears most likely that he first appeared somewhere in Asia. Two distinct species are known to have existed for a time, *homo neanderthalensis*, of inferior intelligence and dexterity, and *homo sapiens*, from which all existing men have come. There may have been other species. The Neanderthal man is believed to have been lost in the struggle for existence, and not to have been absorbed.

Geologists suppose four[12] chief glaciations in Europe, followed by warm periods, the last of which is our present age. Stone implements made by striking off chips appear in the third glaciation and the ensuing warm period. During the fourth glaciation tools and weapons were made by pressure-chipping, and animals were painted upon the ceilings of caves. With the beginning of the fourth warm interval, the geological age in which we now live, some 8000 or 10,000 years B.C., comes the last of the prehistoric periods, extending down to the beginning of written records, at about 3000 B.C. The whole period covered by this pre-history may be not less than 50,000 years.

---

[12] The minor advances of ice are recognised by some geologists in such a way as to bring the number up to six or seven.

Manner of Life

In his early stages man must have been a "gatherer," like the unknown people who left the "kitchen-middens," heaps of oyster-shells, on the coast of Denmark, or the recently extinct "Strandloopers" of the South African coast, or certain modern Negritos. He fed himself by collecting all sorts of easily obtained and immediately available food, both vegetable and animal.

But increase of population made this difficult no doubt, and he had to seek his sustenance with greater energy and intelligence, and at greater risk, than by mere foraging; he therefore took to hunting and fishing. While men were thus employed, women continued to forage, or scratched the ground with sticks and planted the seeds of desirable plants, or adapted certain useful animals to a life of domesticity, thus laying the foundations of agriculture. But crops were uncertain, and at any time they might have to be abandoned to enemies.

Then came the invention of the hoe, and later still the plough, a large hoe which could be hitched to an animal and guided by a strong man. The products of the food-plants now became much more important; and it was worth while for the men to remain at home and till the soil, and care for the animals which could be made to work or to yield food or clothing. In this way many more people could live within a given area. But now also it became necessary to find good land, in competition with others, and to hold it against all comers, after it had been made arable. Thus arose settlements and communities, with property rights and vested interests.

But the supply of land suitable for agriculture was not sufficient for all. Those who could not possess themselves of such land, took a portion of the useful animals and drove them out into the steppes and prairies, moving about as the grass was exhausted or dried up. The animals increased rapidly, without any effort on the part of their owners. But a great deal of

this bad land was necessary for such a life; and, although
one had no improved land or house to defend, one had
to be mobile and enduring, intelligent and resourceful,
in finding pasturage throughout the year, and in
defending the herds and the pasturage-rights against
competitors.

HERDSMEN AND HUSBANDMEN

Although many contined, as they do to this day, to
forage, hunt, and fish, the more progressive at the
beginning of the prehistoric age, 8000 or 10,000 B.C.,
had come to be keepers of flocks or tillers of the soil.
Thus arose two types of living which produced two very
distinct types of character. The peasant had to be
patient, industrious, foresighted, and thrifty; but the
nomadic herdsman needed to be independent,courageous,
warlike, and crafty. The peasant was attached to his
country, the nomad to his tribe. The peasant sought
peace and stability, the nomad freedom and change.
The peasant laid the foundations of civilisation, the
nomad kept alive the ideals of chivalry. The peasant
regarded the nomad with fear, and the nomad looked
upon the peasant with contempt. From the beginning
there was conflict between the two ways of life,
especially as the nomad frequently invaded the domain
of the peasant and carried off his flocks and herds, or
his grain, or his rude manufactures.

In the course of time a people subjected to the
demands of life in the deserts and steppes must become
very different in physical and mental constitution, as
they become diverse in their manners and customs,
from a people which occupies the fertile land. Individuals who survive childhood and succeed in finding
mates and having children in the one case are not of the
same type as those in the other. The community as a
whole gradually assumes the character of those individuals who are best adapted to the particular environment and mode of life. As specialisation continues,

there are fewer and fewer children resembling the un-
desirable types, until at last there are scarcely any, or
perhaps none at all. Thus the Turks remain essentially
an invading people, with the virtues and weaknesses
of Tatar nomads. The Gypsies have been able to
settle nowhere except in Hungary, and there to only a
limited extent. They have no respect for property,
but their loyalty to family is exemplary. Arabs pass
from nomadic to settled life, but they bear the stamp of
the desert for many generations. To this day the
burden of Arabic song and story is the valour, and
freedom, and hospitality of the wilderness.

Nomads do, however, become peasants. The Fertile
Crescent has been replenished again and again from
Arabia, or from the European or Asiatic steppes via
Persia. The reverse also may happen, as when the
South Arabian tribes migrated northward after the
supposed breaking of the great dam at Ma'rib.

ANTIQUITY OF SPEECH

Man must have possessed the faculty of speech before
his dispersion began, for otherwise we should have to
suppose that he acquired it independently in the various
groups, a thing difficult to believe. And if he possessed
the faculty of speech he must, of course, have spoken,
and he must have had a language. It is useless to try
to trace any of the historically known languages or
language-families back to this remote time. Possibly
some one of the known types, such as the monosyllabic-
isolating, may be more closely related to it than others.
Whatever it was, we may be sure that it began very
simply with interjectional elements, such as monkeys
use, and imitative words, such as we still use in English
to describe noises: "rustle," "crackle," "bang," "thud,"
"swish," "pop," "puff." Then came perhaps the
symbolic or suggestive words, such as our English
"bubble," "trouble," "muddle," "huddle," "strike,"
"slap," "beat." Imitative words seem appropriate

because they reproduce the auditory image of the external phenomenon; symbolic words, because they reproduce the kinesthetic (muscle-sensation) image of some act similar to the external phenomenon. The language of sound was accompanied by gesture and grimace, often essential to its intelligibility. Sometimes the gestures predominated, and could be used exclusively, as among Amerind tribes of different spoken tongues. This speech changed rapidly from generation to generation, as is the case to-day in the Amazon country. When first known to us man has well defined types of speech unrelated to each other as far as we may judge. He must therefore have begun to use the known families of speech long before 3000 B.C., even admitting the great and rapid changes of speech in its early stages.

TYPES OF SPEECH

Various attempts have been made to classify the languages of the earth into families. After disposing of certain great groups, such as the Aryan, Semitic, Hamitic, Ugro-Altaic, and Malay-Polynesian, so many unrelated languages remain that original diversity rather than original unity appears to underlie them. They may, however, be grouped according to type of structure.

After various attempts by Schlegel, Grimm, Bopp, Pott, and Schleicher, this scheme was adopted and is still generally accepted:

1. Monosyllabic isolating.
2. Agglutinative.
3. Inflectional.
4. Analytic.

It is supposed that all speech began as No. 1, and that 2, 3 and 4 are successive steps in its development. Tucker[13] has suggested a better scheme:

[13] *The Natural History of Language*, 1908, pp. 93 ff.

I. Inorganic or positional.
II. Organic.
    A. Inflectional.
        1. Amalgamating, without internal change.
           (*a*) Synthetic.
           (*b*) Analytic.
        2. Amalgamating, with internal change.
           (*a*) Synthetic.
           (*b*) Analytic.
        3. Agglutinative.
           (*a*) Suffix.
           (*b*) Prefix.
           (*c*) Suffix-prefix.
           (*d*) Pronoun incorporating.
    B. Holophrastic.

Jespersen[14] has objected to the traditional theory of evolution, just mentioned, showing that Chinese was once less inorganic (structureless) than at present, and that inflection belonged to Aryan languages from the very beginning. Certain it is that pure examples of any of the types are hard to find. They shade off into one another. The origin and inter-relation of the types is not clear. They do not correspond closely to racial groups. White men speak amalgamating (inflected) languages, with internal change (as in Hamitic, Semitic) or without it (as in Aryan), and tending to become more and more synthetic as time goes on. But, whereas Aryan has always been inflected, Hamitic at least at times is agglutinative, and all Hamitic-Semitic speech may have so originated. Black men and Yellow men speak inorganic and agglutinative languages. The Amerind offshoot of the Yellow race used many independent languages, markedly holophrastic, as nowhere else in the world. Apparently there is a racial quality behind Aryan as behind Amerind speech.

[14] *Language*, 1922, Ch. XIX.

Most men speak inorganic and agglutinative (from inorganic?) tongues, Hamitic-Semitic began as agglutinative (with internal change) and became amalgamating.

Such generalisations, while interesting, are dangerous. Perhaps all that may be safely said is this:

1. The earliest speech everywhere was inorganic. Languages of this type still exist, e.g. in China and the Sudan. They are fundamentally monosyllabic, but tend to form compounds. There are no parts of speech, but certain words come to be used as "empty" or relationship-words. Words are invariable in form, but musical tones or cadences are attached to them to differentiate them from homonyms. Word-order is employed as a substitute for inflections or relationship-words.

2. In some communities the relationship-words became more numerous and more specialised. Fixed word-order thus became less necessary, and therefore declined. More compounds were formed. Word-tone thus became less necessary and declined. Parts of speech were differentiated by the attachment of different relationship-words, which however did not fuse with them. Vowel-harmony of all the syllables of such a compound often developed as a means of marking off the group. This is agglutinative speech. It survives, e.g., in the Bantu tongues (prefixing type) and in Turkish (suffix type, with vowel-harmony).

Both the inorganic and agglutinative types are highly variable, because so many different relationship words may come and go with changing fashions of speech. It is much more difficult to detect relationship between actual members of such a group than, e.g., when dealing with amalgamating or inflected languages. For this reason membership in the Aryan or Semitic group is easily recognised; while in the Hamitic group it is more difficult, and in the Turanian group or Amerind group,

often impossible to see any resemblance but general
likeness of structure.

3. The Hamitic-Semitic group carried agglutination
so far that the relationship-words fused at last with the
chief words to which they were affixed or prefixed, and
speech became amalgamating. A word with all its
limiting additions came to be an inseparable unit, no
longer capable of analysis and recombination. At the
same time words were systematically modified by internal
vowel-change, to give regular alterations of meaning,
or application.

4. The Aryan group cannot be shown ever to have
passed through an agglutinative stage. In its original,
isolating stage it spontaneously developed symbolic
changes to indicate alterations of meaning or application. These were, unlike the Hamitic-Semitic, mostly
external suffixes, not internal vowel changes, and
completely dominated the language, instead of being
limited to the characterisation of broad categories.
"Inflectional" is a better term than "amalgamating"
to apply to this type of speech, which seems to spring
directly from some mental habit of the original Aryan
community.

5. Amalgamation was carried so far in the Amerind
languages that all the originally separate elements of
the sentence were run together into a single word.
The sentence and the word thus being identical, the
sentence was incapable of analysis and recombination.

6. Languages of the amalgamating (Hamitic-Semitic)
and the inflectional (Aryan) type tend to rely more
and more upon such relationship-words and word-order
as they may possess, and increasingly to neglect the
word-forms by which they may express relations and
qualifications. They tend thus to approach, in this
final analytic stage, the condition of the most primitive,
inorganic speech. Practically the difference is, of
course, that the broken-down languages always exhibit

some inflection, and that their vocabulary consists, not of monosyllables with inherent tone, but unwieldly polysyllables with an evident history behind them. Persian was originally as highly inflected as Sanskrit, but it was simplified by contact with the alien Parthian and Arabic, and became at last as structureless as English. Nevertheless the irregularity of the "principal parts" of the verbs shows that its present condition is the result of decay.

SPEECH-SOUNDS AND RACE

As speech is a part of culture, and therefore not necessarily connected with race, it would seem that the speech-sounds employed by a community would have no bearing upon its racial character. If peoples learn alien languages, forgetting their own, they presumably learn the necessary alien sounds also. No one now believes that children are born with any special equipment for the production of the sounds required by the social community in which their lot is cast.

It is probably true that racial selection has not specialised the speech-organs of any human group. Infants of any group would, and do, learn perfectly the language of any other group *if introduced under the same conditions as native infants*: i.e. without any alien social heritage or continued alien contacts. But languages are seldom learned in that way, even by individuals, and never by communities. When a community changes its speech, because it invades or is invaded, or is influenced by a cultural drift, there is always a more or less extended period of time during which the old speech is replaced by the new one. In spite of all that has been said to the contrary,[14] the influence of the old sound-habits upon the foreign sounds as finally mastered, is easily seen in groups as in individuals. Yiddish-speaking communities—and this is true to some extent of every foreign group in American cities—are gradually changing over to English, individually and collectively.

The overlapping and the contacts with the community are such that strange counterfeits and substitutes are created and perpetuated. When there are many groups the combined effect is one of degradation or simplification, everything being cancelled that is difficult to any one of the groups. Thus we now hear in New York City a kind of Russian-German-English as well as English robbed of its peculiar niceties and distinctions of sound and sense. Rarely does an individual escape the contamination of his alien origin. The influence even spreads to the community at large, at least in its lower levels. At last it enters the public schools in the persons of poorly paid teachers, and is there promulgated among children of non-alien stock. If we had no other evidence than this we might rightly conclude that the city had been invaded by powerful alien influences, which means primarily an influx of alien blood.

A community may therefore take on a foreign language without taking over its sounds. In fact, it never does take over its sounds unchanged. The learning of sounds lags far behind the learning of the language in other respects. At length there is no longer contact with the original speakers of the pure idiom, but only contact with the contaminated ones. Phonology thus does bear directly upon the racial constitution of a population, and is an index of the extent and character of its racial contamination. The Akkadian (Babylonian-Assyrian) language reveals a marked inability to pronounce the characteristic Semitic sounds, and a tendency to confuse them. It has every appearance of being Semitic in the mouth of half-breed Sumero-Babylonians. The Aramaic dialects are remarkable for their phonetic decay, as we should expect them to be when we reflect that they were spoken by very mixed populations over wide areas.

Morphology, Syntax and Race

Along with phonetic contamination and decay go corresponding changes in the forms of a language and its constructions. What has been said about the sounds of New York English, about Akkadian and Aramaic, holds also of their inflections and syntax. The change of Old Persian, a highly inflected language, to Pahlavi (Middle Persian), an extremely simple one, must be ascribed to the influence of Turanians during the Parthian period. When we find that the Celtic languages of the British Isles, particularly in their spoken forms, differ from all other Aryan languages, and in a way to suggest the Hamitic or Semitic tongues, we shall not be wrong in believing that somehow they have been distorted by foreigners in the process of learning them, and that the foreigners were somehow connected with the Hamitic-Semitic culture, and therefore probably with the Hamitic-Semitic people.

Phonetic Symbols and Transliteration

In the following chapters there will necessarily be some discussion of speech-sounds, and for this certain convenient and unequivocal symbols must be employed. They are those of the International Phonetic Association. When words or word-elements (not sounds) of foreign languages are discussed they are represented in their conventional orthography, or, if Oriental, in the conventional transliteration employed by modern scholars. For reference when reading the subsequent chapters a complete list of all the symbols is given here together with examples, as far as possible from English, French and German.

LIST OF SYMBOLS

b p f w m d t z s n l g k h as in English.

ð or **ḏ** (Semitic) the **th**–sound in "this."

ꝺ or **ṯ** (Semitic) the **th**–sound in "thin."

ʒ the **z**–sound in "azure."

dʒ or **ǧ** the **j**–sound in "joy."

ʃ or **š** the **sh**–sound in "shin."

j the **y**–sound in "yet."

ʔ or **ᴖ** or **ꞌ** the hiatus in "a apple."

r the trilled **r**–sound in Scots "ring."

ç or **ś** the **ch**–sound in German "ich," just behind the teeth.

x or **ẖ** the **ch**–sound in German "ach," back in the mouth.

ɡ or **ġ** the **g**–sound in North German "wegen," corresponding to **x**.

ʁ or **ḥ** the **ch**–sound in Swiss German "ich" and "ach," far back in the mouth.

ɟ or **ḏ** (Egyptian) the **g**–sound in vulgar French "gai,' approaching a **dy**–sound.

c or **ṯ** (Egyptian) the **qu**–sound in vulgar French "qui," approaching a **ty**–sound.

β or **bh** the **w**–sound in South German "was," between a **v**–sound and **w**–sound.

φ or **f** (Egyptian) or **ph** the **f**–sound in South German "pfund," between an **f**–sound and a **wh**–sound.

ḥ an **h**–sound with raised larynx.

ʕ or **ꞌ** or **ꞌ** an **ah**–sound with raised larynx.

q or **ḳ** a **k**–sound far back in the mouth.

ḍ a **d**–sound with a peculiar **u**–effect.

ṭ a **t**–sound with a peculiar **u**–effect.

ọ̆ or **ḍ** a **ð**–sound with a peculiar **u**–effect.

ꝺ or **ṯ** a **ꝺ**–sound with a peculiar **u**–effect.

ẓ a **z**–sound with a peculiar **u**–effect.

ṣ an **s**–sound with a peculiar **u**–effect.

CHAPTER III.

Mediterraneans, Alpines, Nordics and Finno-Ugrians

Four Racial Stocks

FROM Neolithic times down to the present Europe has been inhabited by four stocks, three of which are specialised forms of the White race, and the fourth a mixture of the White with the Yellow. They are only partly associated with languages.

The first of these is the Mediterranean, sometimes called Iberian or proto-Hamitic. It once occupied southern Italy, Sicily, Corsica, and Sardinia, most of Spain, and the west of France and of the British Isles. The type is short, dark, and long-headed.[15] Its proper speech is lost. Perhaps this was of the Hamitic-Semitic family, at least in the British Isles, where it has left its mark upon insular Celtic (Welsh). The Basque language, a survivor of pre-Aryan days, is certainly not Hamitic, and may be Ligurian. The Iberian inscriptions have not yet been deciphered. This stock was originally the same as the proto-Hamitic in northern Africa.

The second is the Alpine. It occupied central France and the central highlands of Europe. It is short, dark, and short-headed. Its proper speech has been lost. This stock was originally the same as the short-headed (Hittite-Armenian) race in Asia Minor, and came into Europe from the east.

The third is the Nordic. It occupied parts of Europe to the north of the Mediterraneans and intruding Alpines, and west of the Yellow peoples of Asia. It is tall, light, and long-headed. It has kept its ancient speech (Aryan).

[15] Tucker, *op. cit.*, pp. 239 ff.

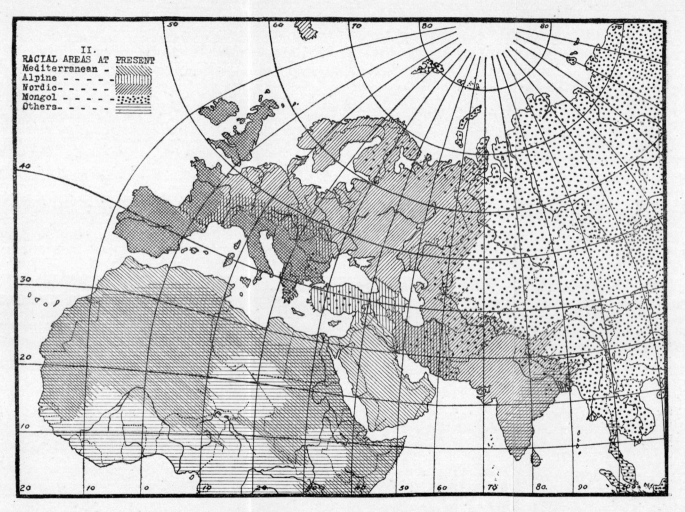

II.
RACIAL AREAS AT PRESENT
Mediterranean -
Alpine - - - - -
Nordic - - - - -
Mongol - - - - -
Others - - - - -

Drawn by Mr. Otto E. Guthe upon the outline map of Mr. Robert B. Hall, both of
the Department of Geography, University of Michigan.

The fourth is the Finno-Ugrian. It occupied a region somewhere between that of the Nordics and that of the purer Yellow peoples, in the north of Eurasia. It is short, dark, and short-headed. It has kept its proper speech (Finno-Ugrian). It has a large element of White (Nordic) blood.

MIXTURES

These four stocks blended where they came into contact, along their frontiers and in the course of their migrations, giving rise to peoples of every variety and degree of combination of racial characteristics.

In Caesar's time Gaul was inhabited by three peoples, "differing in language, customs and laws," but all speaking dialects of the Celtic variety of Aryan speech. The Aquitanians were Mediterraneans, the Gauls were Alpines, and the Belgians were Nordics. Celtic speech was a phase of Aryan, developed in some Nordic community, and spread abroad by the conquests of its speakers. It was the ancient speech of the Belgians, and the adopted speech of the Gauls and Aquitanians. In Spain and Britain also the Belgian Celts imposed their speech upon Mediterranean Iberians. Thus arose three sorts of Celts: Nordic (racially indistinguishable from Germanic), Nordic-Alpine, and Nordic-Mediterranean. With change of language must have gone racial mixture, weaker and weakest in the south and west.[16] This explains why Irishmen are as often tall, brawny, and red, as they are small, delicate, and dark-haired. The French sometimes are indistinguishable from northern Germans, and sometimes have the short heads of the Tyrolese.

Nordics of the Germanic phase of Aryan culture and speech, following in the steps of their Celtic-speaking Nordic brethren, came into contact with Celtic Alpines in the south, Mediterraneans in the west, either spreading

[16] Tucker, *op. cit.*, pp. 241 ff.

their language (southern Germany, Austria, Switzerland, England) or giving it up under the influence of a superior culture (France, Spain).

Nordics of the Slavic phase of Aryan culture and speech were the last to appear in history. They seem to have originated in the eastern part of Nordic territory, as they have a strong infusion of Finno-Ugrian and even of Tatar-Turkish blood. They form the natural transition to the Finno-Ugrian, which is a Yellow stock, profoundly modified by Nordic blood, and speaking languages as profoundly modified by Aryan speech. The Slavs have also been in contact with Tatar-Turkish peoples, and have borne the brunt of Mongol invasion. It is not strange that many Russians, Poles, and Russian-Polish Jews have Mongoloid features with blonde or red hair and blue eyes.

Contact between the White and the Yellow races has been long and intimate. While the Aryan-speaking Persians show strong racial consciousness in their distinction between Iran and Turan, they must have received repeated infusions of Turanian blood. It was through Persia that the Yellow invaders always came. Some of the invading hordes appear to have been undigested mixtures of White and Yellow tribes (Scythian,[17] Parthian[18]). The Sumerians and the Elamites may have been of this mixed ancestry.

White Men's Languages

There is nothing to prevent supposing that the White people of Europe developed at different times many centres of culture and speech. Perhaps Basque and Etruscan, the perplexing languages of the Caucasus, and the extinct tongues of Asia Minor, may be remnants of these early experiments. A common physical type indicates some original community of life and interests, and there may have been at one time a Mediterranean

[17] E. H. Minns in *Ency. Brit.*, xxiv., p. 526.
[18] Ed. Meyer in *Ency. Brit.*, xx, p. 870.

and an Alpine family of languages, just as there certainly was an Aryan and a Finno-Ugrian. Possibly the Alpine race carried with it speech of the extinct Anatolian group, akin to that of the proto-Hittites and proto-Armenians, all forgotten tongues. Probably the Mediterraneans in Europe spoke languages connected more or less remotely with those spoken by Mediterraneans on the opposite shore of Africa. These are well known, though in a very late stage of development.

In the Near East

In the Near East Alpine stock is recognised in contemporary portraits of ancient Hittites, probably of the non-Aryan element whose language has not yet been read. It is strongly represented in certain modern Jews, Armenians, Libanese Syrians, Anatolian Greeks, and Turks; and another variety of it is found in Persia. The Hittites are the only important historical representatives; and they appear to have been ruled by Aryans, at least in the first phase of their civilisation.[19]

It may have been Finno-Ugrian stock that gave to the Sumerians their mildly Mongolian eyes and agglutinative speech, and furnished the Turanian element of the agglomerate Scythic hordes, and the later Scythian-Parthian mixture. But the definitely agglutinative (not inflectional) character of Sumerian, and its vowel-harmony, point to Tatar-Turkish origin.

Mediterranean stock is represented by the Hamitic Egyptians, and their purer relatives, the Libyans. The Semitic branch of this Hamitic stock is, of course, most important in the history of the Near East, as it produced the Semitic Babylonians and Assyrians, the Amorites (Canaanites, Phoenicians, Moabites, Edomites), the Aramaean (Syrian) peoples (including Israel), the South-Arabians (Minaeans, Sabeans), and Abyssinians, and the North-Arabians or Arabs in the narrower sense of the term.

[19] Witzel, *Hethitische Keilschrift-Urkunden*, Fulda, 1924.

There seems to be no doubt that the Aryan tongues originated with the long-headed blonde race of northern Europe. In the west the Aryan-speaking Greeks, (Belgian) Celts, Germans, and Slavs, were blonde. The Aryan element of the Scythians and Parthians may have been so. But the Aryan-speaking Iranians and Indians are far removed from the blonde type, because of mixture with the indigenous peoples of these countries. In Persia these were a variety of the Alpine race. In India they were chiefly Dravidians, a very dark race whose ethnic and linguistic affinities are unknown.

HAMITES AND ARYANS

When the Aryan-speaking Nordics, about 3000 B.C., pressed westward in Europe they encountered different groups of Mediterraneans, possessing a certain culture and speech. They mingled with these peoples and aryanized them, but not without some effect upon the resulting culture and speech. From these peculiarities it is proper to infer the character of the old, pre-Aryan civilisation and language. In the British Isles certain syntactic phenomena of insular Celtic speech have led to the inference that in this region languages were spoken which had some relation, however remote, to the Hamitic-Semitic family. Almost nothing is known of the Celtic speech of ancient Gaul and Spain. Perhaps there were several Mediterranean cultures and speech-families, and the Basque may be descended from a different one of these.

Hamitic and Aryan have certain features in common. Both have the not at all obvious distinction of gender. Human beings and animals, inanimate objects, and even abstract concepts, are assigned to either a masculine or a feminine category, according to actual sex, or fancied sex-qualities (large, small, strong, weak), or for reasons which we can no longer discover, because of the operation of analogy. In Hamitic we know that this grammatical gender arose out of a broader distinction between the large and important and primary, and the small and unimportant and secondary.   In a still earlier stage there was a much larger system of noun-classes (Ful, Bantu).   The third, or neuter, gender is related in the singular to the masculine, and in the plural to the feminine.   How different, *e.g.*, is the Turkish system.   Here there is not only no distinction between nouns (as in Aryan and Hamitic), or between verbs with subjects of different gender (Hamitic); but even in the pronoun there is no such distinction.   There is no difference between "he" and "she."

Both Hamitic and Aryan are inflected, and they are perhaps the only inflected languages of the world, if we except the half-aryanised Finno-Ugrian.   But Hamitic was originally agglutinative, and Egyptian, *e.g.*, remained so to the end, though Aryan probably has always been inflected.

Vowel-gradation (Ablaut) in Aryan is often the result of accent, but not always: Persian has **īn,** "this," **ān,** "that."   Hittite has **eniš,** "this," **anniš,** "that," **uniš,** "that" (far away).   Hamitic has similar symbolic use of vowels,[20] but there is no reason for supposing that there is any relation between the two.

The outstanding difference between Aryan and Hamitic-Semitic tongues is that the former have roots composed of two consonants and an intermediate vowel, while Hamitic-Semitic languages have roots consisting of consonants only: from one to four, usually two (as in Hamitic) or three (as in Hamitic, Semitic).

There is no resemblance whatever between Hamitic and Aryan inflectional elements or vocabulary, excepting loan-words, imitative and symbolic words, and chance correspondencies.

DOLMENS, CROMLECHS AND MENHIRS

These words, derived from the language of Brittany, signify three characteristic varieties of Neolithic monu-

---

[20] Meinhof, *Die Sprachen der Hamiten*, 1912, p. 13.

E

ments: the table, consisting of upright stones and a top, the circle of upright stones, and the single upright stone. It was in France and England that such remains first attracted attention, although they are found along the north African coast and in Palestine. In these places they occur in such numbers as to preclude the possibility of fortuitous origin. Peake[21] thinks they are connected with localities where metals or pearls were to be found, and mark the path of trade undertaken by a certain race of people of well marked characteristics. Sergi[22] thinks they were left by Mediterraneans, who originated in Africa and spread into western Europe. They are more numerous in France (Brittany); the largest of them occurs in England (Stonehenge).

It has been supposed that they were built by Mediterranean people who were ancestors of the Berbers (Libyans) and of the pre-Aryan population of western France and England. The only obstacle to such a theory would be the supposed blonde character of the ancient Libyans and modern Berbers, in view of the dark character of the European Mediterraneans. Since there is only one blonde race on earth, the Nordic, it has seemed necessary to suppose that Celts or Germans brought this strain into Morocco and the Atlas mountains. This difficulty is somewhat relieved by the following considerations:

1. When we meet an unknown people we note those peculiarities which are strange to us, ignoring those which are familiar.[22]

2. We think only of the individuals having these qualities, and not of those individuals who are without them; and report that the strange people are throughout characterised by these qualities.

3. The Egyptians were a very dark people. Not many individuals of even moderately light hair would

[21] *The Bronze Age and the Celtic World*, 1922, Ch. IV.
[22] *The Mediterranean Race*, 1901, Ch. III.

have been required to impress them with the supposed blonde character of a strange race.

4. Egyptian painting is symbolic, not realistic. With the blue-eyed Libyans of their frescoes compare the individuals with red or green eyes.[22] Yellow hair would only mean "lighter than ours."

5. Libyans frequently appeared at Rome, but they excited no comment, because they were much like the Roman people themselves (Mediterranean). On the other hand note the wonder aroused by the blond, blue-eyed Celts and Germans.[22] Evidently the Libyans were not blond or blue-eyed in any such sense, although they might have been as light as Italians occasionally were.

6. Modern Berbers at most have light brown or reddish hair; and often the lighter colour is observed in the beard rather than upon the head.[22]

7. "Bertholon among 344 individuals in the northwest of Tunis, found 2.03 per cent. with blonde and red hair, 9.01 per cent. with intermediate, perhaps chestnut tints, and 88.95 per cent. dark."[22] This is perhaps about the percentage that might be found among European Mediterraneans.

8. The Atlas mountains, where the light type is most often found, reach a height of 12,000 feet above sea level. Here the lighter individuals of a brown-haired Mediterranean people might be more suited to the environment.[22]

It is not impossible then that Libyans, Berbers, Iberians, and the pre-Aryan peoples of western France and Britain were one people, and made the dolmens, cromlechs, and menhirs.

DRUIDISM

The peculiar religious system which the Romans found among Celts in Gaul and Britain[23] is without

---

[23] Caesar, *De Bello Gallico*, VI, 13 ff.

parallel anywhere among Aryan-speaking peoples. A strongly organised priestly class, custodians and teachers of esoteric doctrine (?), administered justice, interpreted the moral code, practised magic and divination, and performed sacrifices. Nevertheless the ancient Aryan gods were known. Caesar was told that the cult centred in Britain. It has been assumed to have had some connection with the Neolithic stone monuments, and with the immediately pre-Aryan people of Gaul and Britain. The invading Celts are supposed to have adopted the religion of the land which they conquered, and to have become subject to its ancient hierarchy. But of all this there is no proof. Druidism may have been a natural development of Celtic beliefs and practices.

PICTS

Britain was twice invaded by Celtic-speaking peoples, first by the Goidels (Q-Celts), then by the Brythons (P-Celts). When the Goidels came they appear to have encountered an older people whom they drove westward; but, upon being themselves hard pressed by the Brythons they allied themselves with the aborigines and later absorbed them. This pre-Celtic race, the Picts of Roman writers, remains enshrouded in great mystery and uncertainty. Rhys[24] says that their speech lingered as late as the sixth century A.D. What that speech was we cannot say. But the Insular Celtic languages, particularly colloquial Welsh, show certain peculiarities unparalleled in Aryan languages, and these remind one strongly of Hamitic and Semitic.

WELSH SYNTAX

The remains of Continental Celtic are very scanty and imperfectly understood. The speech of Brittany (Armorican) does not help, because it is a dialect of Welsh, and not a surviving dialect of Gaulish. We are unable therefore to say whether or not Continental

[24] *Celtic Britain*, 1882, pp. 257 ff.

Celtic was like Latin or other Aryan tongues in its sentence-structure, or whether it partook of the peculiarities of Insular Celtic. But it may be assumed that Celtic was like other Aryan, unless influenced by alien forces. The Insular Celtic is well known through ancient literary monuments and still surviving dialects (Welsh, Erse, Scots-Gaelic, Manx).

Sir John Morris Jones, in an appendix to Rhys and Brynmor-Jones,[25] discusses at length parallels between colloquial Welsh and ancient Egyptian, and other Hamitic speech. The assumption is that when an invading host of men take wives of alien speech the resulting children will learn the tongue of the fathers as spoken by the mothers, and that the resulting dialect will possess certain peculiarities of syntax alien to the former and characteristic of the latter. In spite of Jespersen[26] I see no reason for doubting this possibility. Such a situation would tend at least to corruption and simplification. The other assumption is more difficult. We are supposing that ancient British was the speech of a remote northern branch of a proto-Hamitic race, not a member of the Hamitic family in any narrower sense. Egyptian, on the other hand, is a highly specialised member of the eastern branch of Hamitic, very different indeed from western Hamitic as now represented. Modern Hamitic dialects, and even ancient Egyptian, are too far removed in time from the speech of ancient Britain to justify close comparison.

Using the article by Sir John as a basis, I should venture to state the case thus:

1. The normal sentence begins with its verb: "Read John the book" (John read the book). Should the subject begin the sentence, the subject is really a nominative absolute and very emphatic: "John, (he) read the book" (It was John, and no one else, who read

[25] *The Welsh People*, 1900 and later, App. B.   Cf. Rhys, *op. cit.*

[26] *Op. cit.*, Ch. XI, especially §§ 8, 10.

the book). Found in Welsh, Irish, Egyptian, Arabic, Hebrew.

2. A dependent genitive follows the noun which it qualifies (construct relationship): "Horse-war" (Horse of war). Found in Welsh, Irish, Egyptian, all the Semitic languages. This is a phonetic composite, like Aryan "war-horse," but exactly reversed. When the relationship is expressed by a preposition (Egyptian) or a genitive ending (Arabic) the construction resembles, however, Aryan (English, Latin): "Horse of war," "Equus belli."

3. Pronominal suffixes are added (agglutinatively) to a verbal noun (crude verb form) to produce the verb with inherent subject: "See-he" (He sees). They cannot be used when there is a nominal subject. You say: "See-man" (The man sees). You cannot say: "See-he man" as you do in Latin: "Vidit homo." Found in Welsh, Irish, Egyptian. Welsh and Irish had in addition their old Aryan inflection. The same suffixes may be used to indicate the object: "See-he" (Sees him). Found in Irish and Egyptian. These suffixes are attached to nouns regularly (Egyptian, Arabic) or by exception (Welsh): "Horse-he" (His horse). This is common with nouns which have gradually become prepositions (Welsh, Egyptian, all the Semitic languages): "Top-he" (Above him). The practice is then extended to other prepositions (Welsh, Egyptian, all the Semitic languages): "In-he" (In him). Even demonstrative pronouns may take the suffixes (Welsh, Egyptian, Ethiopic): "That-he" (That which belongs to him).

4. From the above it is evident that "horse-war," "see-he," "see-man," "horse-he," "top-he," "in-he," and "that-he" are identical constructions. They are all substantives with a dependent genitive. The verbal forms consist of a verbal noun and a dependent genitive, which may be understood as subjective or objective, according to circumstances. This use of the verbal

substantive as a finite verb is found in Welsh and Egyptian.

5. Prepositions may be used with a crude verb form (verbal noun) to produce the three cardinal tenses: "I in see" (I see), "I after see" (I saw), "I for see" (I shall see). This is found in Welsh and Irish (cf. "I'm after eating my dinner"), and (excepting the second) in Egyptian.

6. The auxiliary verbal noun "be" is used with the vernal noun (*not* the participle) of the principle verb in numerous combinations: "Be see-he," "Be-he see-he" (He sees). These are found in Egyptian. A similar construction: "Is answered Owen" (Owen answered) is found in Welsh.

7. The preposition "in" (as above stated) is used to express the present tense. It is also used to express predication: "He in child" (He is a child). This is found in Welsh and Egyptian. The negative of the construction occurs in Arabic. "In it" occurs independently in Arabic and Ethiopic in the sense "there is." "In" converts an adjective into an adverb: "In quick" (Quickly). This construction is found in Welsh and Egyptian. Irish parallels every one of these, quite independently.

8. Objects which present themselves to the mind primarily as a mass, rather than as separate, are designated by a collective noun from which the singular (noun of unity) is formed by a special suffix. This device is found in Welsh and Arabic.

CHAPTER IV.

Hamites and Semites

HAMITIC STRAIN IN AFRICA

IN north-western, eastern, and extreme southern Africa are peoples speaking languages with characteristics which mark them off sharply from other African tongues.[27] [28] Examination of these peoples reveals in many cases a White strain which may be assumed to belong to the language. The Sahara was once occupied by people of the Mediterranean race; and they migrated southward into the Horn of East Africa, into equatorial Africa, and even to the Cape. Thus arose the following Hamitic and Hamitoid groups: (1) Negroid Hamites, of primitive speech, western Sudan; (2) Purer Hamites, of Libyan speech, northern Sahara; (3) Less pure Hamites, of speech more nearly Semitic, along the Nile valley; (4) Less pure Hamites, of Cushitic speech, in the Horn of eastern Africa; (5) Strongly Negroid Hamites, of Negroid speech, lake region of eastern Africa; (6) Bushman-like Hamites, of Bushman-like speech, extreme southern Africa; (7) Proto-Hamitic and Sudanic fusion, speaking Bantu languages, equatorial Africa.

WHITE AFFINITIES

Hamitic languages have grammatical gender (or an older, more elaborate system leading to it), and vowel-gradation, which are features possessed only by Semitic

---

[27] Not counting the Semitic languages which are intruders from Asia.

[28] Meinhof, *op. cit.*, and *An Introduction to the Study of African Languages*, 1915.

and Aryan. They are mostly inflected, but were once probably agglutinative. The languages of the true Negroes (Sudanians), on the other hand, are not inflected, but are monosyllabic in principle, with word-tone, like Chinese. They have no gender. The genitive is placed before its governing noun. Bushman languages are characterised by their "clicks" or vacuum-sounds produced by the tongue against parts of the mouth. Bantu languages have elaborate classification of the noun, a system probably borrowed from very ancient Hamitic (Ful type), and make extensive use of prefixes.

RESEMBLANCE TO SEMITIC

Not only do the Hamitic tongues differ essentially from the other languages of Africa, and resemble in general the speech of other groups of White men (Semitic, Aryan), but they are so similar to Semitic that a very close relationship must have existed with that group. Semitic appears to be rather a development of Hamitic, because the former may far more easily have grown out of the latter than the reverse. Semitic is a specialised form of Hamitic, in which agglutination has given way to inflection. The outline of the accidence has assumed a more definite form. Roots, with few exceptions, have become triliteral. Many obscure and sporadic phenomena in Semitic are clear in Hamitic and part of its essential structure. The western and southern Hamitic languages are least like Semitic. The Semitic dialects of Abyssinia are supposed to have been brought from South Arabia via Bab al-Mandeb within historical times not very remote. They have come into contact with Hamitic and true Negro (Sudanian) languages, and show the influence of these. Aside from such influence they appear in some respects to occupy a position midway between Hamitic and Semitic. It has even been thought that they are native to African soil.

NUMERALS[29]

Three successive stages in the art of counting are represented by (1) Egyptian, (2) Ethiopic and Akkadian (Assyrian, Babylonian), and (3) other Semitic languages. In Egyptian about half the digits have names[30] corresponding to their names in Semitic, and the highest common term is the highest of the digits, **md̲,** "ten." In Ethiopic and Akkadian (Semitic) all the digits have their common Semitic names, and so do all the tens and hundreds, with some variation in the form and manner of composition, and the highest common term is still **m't** (=**md̲**); but the word now means "a hundred," the highest of the tens, instead of "ten," the highest of the digits. Ethiopic uses another word, **elef,** in the sense of "a very large number," "a myriad." The other Semitic languages (except Akkadian) have gone a step further, and given this word the meaning of "a thousand," the highest of the hundreds.[31]

This means that Hamites and Semites, before their separation, counted as far as "ten" only. When the Ethiopic and Akkadian groups split off, the Semites counted as far as "a hundred" only. Before the so-called Canaanitish migration (c. 2500 B.C.) they counted to "a thousand."

The correctness of this supposition is supported by certain familiar peculiarities in all the Semitic languages. Arabic has a singular number, a dual, a lesser plural (up to "ten"), and a greater plural. With the numerals "three" to "ten" the old Hamitic dualism and law of polarity operate so as to place the numeral in the gender opposite that of the thing numbered. This law does not apply to numbers above "ten," which were filled in after the separation of Hamites and Semites. From "eleven" to "ninety-nine" another construction is used,

---

[29] Discussed by the present writer in *Papers of the Michigan Academy of Science, Arts and Letters*, Vol. VI, 1926.

[30] Originally fanciful names for the fingers?

[31] Noticed by Grimme, *Mohammed*, 1904, p. 7.

and from "a hundred" upward, still another construction, as though here also two further stages of development were represented.

ATTITUDE OF SEMITISTS

Semitic scholars have uniformly maintained an attitude of doubt as to the character and direction of the undeniable relationship between Hamitic and Semitic, holding that Semitic grammatical structure and morphology were widely borrowed by different groups of Africans, the most conspicuous example being Egyptian. They leave one to suppose that the borrowers were Negroes, and they take no account of the Hamitic stock. Perhaps they imply that Hamitic blood came from Arabia, along with the borrowed Semitic speech.

PRESSURE ARTICULATION[32]

The "pressure-articulation" is a wide-spread peculiarity of Hamitic and Semitic speech. In its primary form it consists of a closure of the glottis and upward motion of the larynx toward the rigid base of the tongue, in addition to the main articulation which is in progress. By this forcible elevation of the larynx air pressure is created for the explosive (**p, t, k,** etc.) and fricative (**f, s,** etc.) sounds which are usually made with air-pressure from the lungs; and the following vowel begins with a "snap," and a "pinched" sound due to the contracted condition of the throat. In this way the **p** is followed first by a hiatus, **ʔ,** and then by **ʕ**. The last element is called the "pressure-tone," and it is identical with the sound of the Arabic letter ع and the Hebrew letter **y**. The complete sound of such a **p** would thus be **pʔʕ**. Then also, because the back of the tongue has been raised by the upward pressure, the succeeding vowel has a u-resonance, even though it be an **a** or an **i**. Some Hamitic languages have, and

[32] Based upon the work of Professor Meinhof. See *Zeitschrift für Eingeborenen-Sprachen*, 1920–21, XI, pp. 81 ff.

probably all once had, peculiar explosives and fricatives of this kind. When we turn to Semitic languages we find another sort of pressure-articulation which seems to have grown out of the first. It is applied to a limited number of consonants only, the so-called "emphatic" sounds. It consists of upward pressure of the larynx, without any closure of the glottis, and therefore without any explosion of the glottis after the principal articulation. In ancient Hebrew this pressure was still sufficient to change the resonance of near-by consonants. In Aramaic pressure-tone occasionally superceded the principal articulation, and changed, e.g. **ardˀˤā** into **arˤā** or even **arqā**. In Arabic nothing remains but a u-resonance of the consonants, which changes the resonance of near-by consonants and vowels. These then are the so-called "emphatic" dentals and sibilants of Hebrew and Arabic. They are not actually louder than ordinary sounds, but they seem to the speaker to be so, because he is sensible of the greater effort used in producing them. The pressure tone, ˤ, and its voiceless counterpart, **ḥ**, occur independently (Arabic ع, ح, Hebrew ע, ח). The old emphatic **kˀˤ** became **q** through the raising of the tongue (Hebrew ק, Arabic ق).

It is evident that Hamitic and Semitic possess in common a very unusual articulation, and that this articulation is inseparable from primitive Hamitic and Semitic speech.

DICHOTOMY AND GENDER IN HAMITIC LANGUAGES

Meinhof[33] discovered in the Hamitic languages a fundamental division of objects into two classes: (1) Persons, big things, subjects, males; (2) things, small things, objects, females. This is a simplification of a larger scheme of four classes: (1) Persons, (2) things,

[33] *Op. cit.*, and *Das Ful in seiner Bedeutung für die Sprachen der Hamiten, Semiten, und Bantu, Zeitschrift der deutschen morgenländischen Gesellschaft,* LXV.

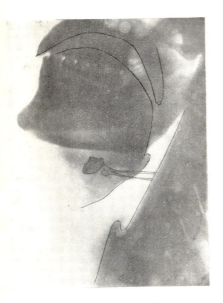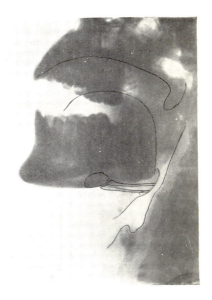

PRESSURE ARTICULATION.

X-ray photographs of a native of Aleppo, northern Syria, taken by Dr. G. Panconcelli-Calzia, Hamburgisches Kolonialinstitut, outlined by Mr. W. L. Cristanelli, University of Michigan, published by present writer in *Vox*, 1914, 82 ff. No. 1 shows position of organs during ordinary breathing. No. 2 shows position of organs during pressure-articulation. Larynx is pulled upward and pharynx contracts, tongue rises in consequence, uvula is pulled up as when making vowels.

(3) big things, (4) small things—still observed by the Ful language. Bantu, which Meinhof believes to be descended from a very early blending of Hamitic with Sudanian, has many noun-classes, each with its own plural ending and its special pronoun. The characteristically Hamitic dichotomy, or two-fold division, in language is only a part of a general dichotomy of thinking. All objects of thought are assignable to one or the other of two classes. Tertium non datur. The first consists of primary, or relatively important, the second of secondary, or relatively unimportant, things. Gradually the first class comes to be associated with the masculine, and the second class with the feminine, and grammatical gender arises; but the gender is still movable, and the same object may be thought of as either masculine or feminine according to circumstances. "Cow" is masculine when it means a living, milk-giving, bovine, but feminine when it means "beef." Big things are masculine and small things are feminine, regardless of actual sex. The sign of the object of a verb, **t**, gradually becomes the general sign of the feminine. In short, grammatical gender indicates "primary" and "secondary," not actual gender or sex.

Dichotomy and Gender in Semitic Languages

In Semitic languages feminine endings do not always represent females. The numerals "three" to "ten" are given the feminine endings in order to subordinate them to masculine nouns. Corresponding with masculine singulars there is in Arabic a set of feminine abstracts or collectives which serve as plurals; and from masculine collectives a singular may be formed by adding the feminine ending. A verbal noun is made to indicate a single instance of action by the addition of the feminine ending. An adjective may be intensified in the same way. In all these cases the feminine gender is the sign of the secondary class.

GENDER IN ARYAN LANGUAGES

In Aryan languages nothing of this kind occurs. There are three genders: (1) Masculine, (2) feminine, and (3) neuter. It is true that Aryan resembles Hamitic and Semitic in having gender at all. The neuter appears to have been made up out of the masculine and feminine, so that there were in Aryan also originally only two genders, masculine and feminine. But these do not appear to have originated out of the notion of "primary" and "secondary," nor of "male" and "female." Certain declensions happened to have many words in them which denoted females or males, and sex came to be associated with them.

POLARITY IN HAMITIC LANGUAGES

Associated with dichotomy Meinhof[34] found another principle which he calls "polarity." If one coating of a Leyden jar is positively electrified the opposite coating will be found to be negative, and vice versa. If one end of a steel bar is made N-magnetic the other becomes S-magnetic, and vice versa. There are two conditions and two positions, and therefore only two possible ways of associating the conditions and positions. If an object must be thought of as belonging to one of two classes, the secondary aspect of that object, or whatever is contrasted with that object, must be put in the remaining class. Contrast must be maintained. The change from one to the other is the important thing. The sign of that change may come to indicate exactly opposite conditions. In Nama (Hottentot) and Somali the plural of a masculine noun is feminine, while in Somali the plural of a feminine noun is masculine. Polarity is carried so far in social usage that boys belong to their mother's, girls to their father's, family. Before initiation into the rights of manhood and womanhood the candidates for a time must wear the clothing of the opposite sex. A woman once became "chief" of a tribe, whereupon her husband became officially the "wife." [35]

Polarity in Semitic Languages

The numerals "three" to "ten" are placed in the gender opposite that of the thing numbered by them. This familiar rule of Hebrew and Arabic grammar is ordinarily explained as an effort to maintain a contrast between the numeral and its noun, or to emphasise the substantive character of the numeral: "a (feminine) triad of men," "a (masculine) pentad of women." The numeral is made feminine to subordinate it to its masculine noun; but, if it must be used with a feminine noun, it must be placed in the class opposite to the feminine, which is the masculine.

As we have just seen, in Arabic masculine singulars are contrasted with feminine collectives which serve them as plurals; and masculine collectives are contrasted with feminine nouns of unity which serve them as singulars.

A masculine adjective may be intensified by making it feminine: **karīm, karīma,** "noble," "more noble." Perhaps we have the opposite of this in **ḫalīfa,** "successor (feminine)" to the Prophet.

The feminine collectives, twice mentioned above as being used with masculine singulars in the manner of plurals, are called in Arabic grammar "broken" or "inner" plurals because they appear to be reconstructed out of the consonants of the singulars without reference to the form of the singulars. In reality they are not made from the singulars, but they are independent forms associated with singulars. And the precise form chosen is the one which will in each case produce the best contrast. The Arabic broken plurals may be classified with respect to the principle of contrast as follows:[36]

1. When the singular has *short* vowels only, the

---

[34] *Op. cit.*   [35] Meinhof, *Die Sprachen der Hamiten,* p. 20, note 1.

[36] Taken from my article in *The American Journal of Semitic Languages and Literatures,* XLI, 179 ff.

plural has a *long* vowel; the other factors are immaterial:

kalb—kilāb
ğamal—ğimāl
ʿabd—ʿabīd
qalb—qulūb
ğund—ğunūd
haġar—hiġāra [with fem. ending -a(tun)]
ʿamm—ʿumūma [with fem. ending -a(tun)]
šaih—mašā'ih [with nominal prefix ma-]
husn—mahāsin [with nominal prefix ma-]

2. When the singular has a *long* vowel, the plural has *short* vowels only; the other factors are immaterial:

kitāb—kutub
qadīb—qudub
rasūl—rusul
tāġir—tuġur
kāmil—kamala [with fem. ending -a(tun)]
ʾamīr—ʾumarāʾ [with fem. ending -āʾ(u)]
ġarīh—ġarhā [with fem. ending -ā]
bāhil—buhhal [with doubling of second radical]

3. When the singular has a *certain* vowel, the plural has a *different* one of the same length:

šarīf—širāf
himār—hamīr
falak—fuluk

4. When the singular has a certain vowel in a *certain position*, the plural has it in *another position*:

sāhib—sihāb
kātib—kuttāb [with doubling of second radical]

5. When the singular is *without* the intensive prefix ʾa-, the plural is formed *with* it:

bahr—ʾabhur
riğl—ʾarğul
qufl—ʾaqful
ğabal—ʾağbul
sabuʿ—ʾasbuʿ

farḫ—ʾafriḥa [with fem. ending -a(tun)]
zirr—ʾazirra [with fem. ending -a(tun)]
burǧ—ʾabriǧa [with fem. ending -a(tun)]
raǧīf—ʾarǵifa [with fem. ending -a(tun)]
qarīb—ʾaqribāʾ [with fem. ending -āʾ(u)]
ḫabar—ʾaḫbār [with the long vowel for the short]

6. When the singular is formed *with* the intensive prefix ʾa-, the plural is formed *without* it:

ʾazraq—zurq
ʾawwal (for ʾaʾwal)—ʾuwal

7. When the singular is *without* the feminine endings -a(tun), -āʾ(u), or -ā, the plural is formed *with* them:

qird—qirada
qadīm—qudamāʾ
nabī—ʾanbijāʾ
mait—mautā

See also the many mixed forms above, in which this law is operative.

8. When the singular is formed *with* the feminine endings -a(tun) or -āʾu, the plural is formed *without* them:

ramala—ramal
ḥalqa—ḥalaq
qiṣṣa—qiṣaṣ
ʿulba—ʿulab
zarqāʾ—zurq

In (1) and (2), in (5) and (6), and in (7) and (8) the same device is used with exactly opposite values. In (3) and in (4) we see the principle of contrast. Both may finally be considered as resting upon the principle of contrast maintained between the two members of a two-class system.

Arabic possesses a number of animal and other names in which **ibn** (son of—) is compounded with some descriptive word. The plurals of these are all made with the word **banāt** (daughters of—), in the gender

F

opposite that of the singular, and without any regard for the actual sex of the object:

> **ibn dā'ir,** "son of lewd," "young stallion camel"
>
> **ibn a'waǧ,** "son of Crooked," "offspring of Crooked, a celebrated stallion"
>
> **ibn labūn,** "son of full-uddered (mother),""young male camel"
>
> **ibn āwā,** "son of wow-wow," "jackal"
>
> **ibn awbar,** "son of hairy," "bad mushroom"
>
> **ibn na'š,** "son of Great Bear," "star of Ursa Major "

Evidently the broken plurals are feminine, not only because they are abstracts and collectives, but because they must be polaric opposites to their masculine singulars.

In the imperfect of the verb the inferiority sign, **t**, distinguishes the second person from the first, and the feminine from the masculine. "You" is secondary to "I," and "she" is secondary to "he."

Reversal of the tenses, as described just below, may be a polaric phenomenon.

Relative Time

Aryan languages express both the absolute and the relative time of an action:

Absolute: (1) Past, (2) Present, (3) Future.

Relative: (a) Complete, (b) Incomplete, (c) Indefinite.

Examples:

> 1a. "He had written."
>
> 1b. "He was writing."
>
> 1c. "He wrote."
>
> 2a. "He has written."
>
> 2b. "He is writing."
>
> 2c. "He writes."
>
> 3a. "He will have written."
>
> 3b. "He will be writing."
>
> 3c. "He will write."

Hamitic and Semitic languages, for the most part, express only the relative time of an action. There are but two "tenses," and either may be used for an action in any of the three grand divisions of time, according to the speaker's conception of the act, as finished or still going on.

In Hebrew a narrative begun with one form must be continued with the other:

"The scribe (had) taken the book, and (was) opening it, and (was) saying," i.e. "The scribe took the book, and opened it, and said."

"The scribe (will be) taking the book, and (will have) opened it, and (will have) said," i.e. "The scribe will take the book, and will open it, and say."

The first of these is rational enough. The second, however, appears to be a mere polaric reversal of the first, and inexplicable by itself.

Derived Conjugations

In German **schwingen** means "to swing," while **schwenken** means "to cause to swing"; **hangen** and **fallen** mean "to hang" and "to fall," while **hängen** and **fällen** mean "to cause to hang" and "to cause to fall." Intransitives are thus made into transitives, by an instinctive intensification. The velum is pulled upward, and ɲ becomes **k**; or the tongue is pushed forward and upward and **a** becomes ɛ. In both cases the speaker has a muscular sensation of intensity. So the Semitic languages possess an entire "conjugation" in which the second of the three radical consonants is lengthened, or, as some inaccurately say, doubled, to express intensity, or repetition, or transitiveness. Thus **kasara** means "to break," while **kassara** means "to shatter," or "cause to break." In another "conjugation" the first vowel is lengthened to express effort, or rather, to give the speaker the muscular sensation of effort: **qātala**, "to try to kill," **kātaba**, "to write, with effort to reach." All such devices arise naturally,

and may be expected in any language. But in the
Hamitic and Semitic languages three "conjugations,"
or three characteristic modifications of the root, occur
which cannot have arisen independently, and are too
fundamental in both families to have been borrowed
by either.

CAUSATIVE CONJUGATION

A causative verb contains the verb "make" in addition to its essential verbal idea. Hamitic and Semitic
languages regularly employ causative verbs instead of
auxiliary verbs, "make" or "cause." All Semitic
languages have a causative stem with a prefix:

> **sa-** in Minaean; vestiges in Arabic, Ethiopic, and
> Akkadian.
> **ša-** in Akkadian; vestiges in Minaean and Aramaic.
> **ha-** in Hebrew and Aramaic; vestiges in Arabic.
> **ʾa-** in Arabic, Ethiopic and Aramaic.

The original identity of these four prefixes has been
doubted, but I see no reason to do so. Phonetically **s**
may become **ʃ**; **s** may also become **h** (cf. **s**eptem and
hepta); and **h** may become **ʔ**. The historical appearance
of the sounds also roughly follows this order. Akkadian
and Minaean have **s** and **ʃ**; Hebrew has **h**; Aramaic has **ʔ**,
but remembers both **ʃ** and **h**; Ethiopic has **ʔ**, and traces
of **s**; Arabic has **ʔ** and vestiges of both **s** and **h**.

The causative prefix or suffix **s** or **ʃ** is widely distributed in the Hamitic languages, as Meinhof[37] has
shown.

SOCIAL-RECIPROCAL CONJUGATION

In all Semitic languages, with the exception of
Aramaic, there is a conjugation marked by the prefix,
na-, ni-, or **in-.** Its sense is reflexive and passive.
In Hebrew it expresses also social and reciprocal action.

Hamitic prefixes or suffixes **m** or **n** to express social or
reciprocal action, or the state resulting from action.

Habitive-Reflexive Conjugation

There is another conjugation in the Semitic languages, marked by the prefix **ta-** or **t-**, the latter sometimes infixed. Its sense is reflexive, passive, and reciprocal. In Arabic it is also habitive, expressing the state resulting from an action.

Hamitic prefixes or suffixes **t** to express the state resulting from an action, or to express reflexive action. These two conjugations have come to overlap in their functions, both in Hamitic and Semitic. In old Arabic the **in-** conjugation is never indirectly reflexive, and never reciprocal, as is the **t-** conjugation; but this seems to be a later distinction. In modern Arabic both are used for the passive: some verbs preferring one, and some the other.

Their origins and original functions are more clearly seen in Hamitic.

Hamitic uses the signs of these three conjugations very freely, both as prefixes and as suffixes, but does not compound them. Semitic employs them as prefixes only, and in combinations, completely fused. Hamitic therefore appears to represent older conditions of structure.

Aryan, Hamitic and Semitic Roots

Roots, in Aryan, Hamitic, and Semitic languages, are pure abstractions of the philologist. From comparison of many actual forms he isolates the significant element common to all, and supposes that it expresses the abstract idea behind all the concrete examples taken from usage.

Aryan roots are typically composed of two consonants with a certain vowel between, such as **LAB** or **GEN**. In striking contrast to these are the roots of Hamitic and Semitic, which are composed of one or more consonants, without any vowels, such as **KTB** or **KSR**. The root-idea inheres in these consonants.

[37] *Zeitschrift für Eingeborenen-Sprachen,* 1922, XII, pp. 241 ff.

To be pronounced they must, of course, receive vowels; and the vowels then express the particular application or limitation of the root-idea. Hamitic and Semitic are thus very much closer to one another structurally than either of them is to Aryan.

But there is a typical difference between Hamitic and Semitic. The former has generally roots with two consonants, while the latter has generally roots with three. Yet both will tolerate words having more or less than the typical number. The question is: Have the biliterals been reduced or the triliterals increased?

ORIGIN OF TRICONSONANTAL ROOTS

A survey of all the Hamitic languages reveals comparatively few roots that have become biliteral through the loss of a third radical. The biliteral root is typical and original. This may become quadriliteral by the simple process of reduplication: **BRBR** from **BR** (in Bilin); or triliteral by a partial reduplication **LQQ** from **LQ** (in Bilin). Sometimes a prefix or suffix may have fused with the root, and no longer be recognisable as such: In Semitic we find **ŠLHB** from **LHB** (in Syriac), **HRWQ** from **RWQ** (in Arabic), **TLMD** from **LMD** (in Arabic), **BRZL** from **BRZ** (in Hebrew). Two roots may be united and used as one: **KT-HM** (Kafa). In Semitic they are always fused under such circumstances: **DHRG** from **DHR** and **HRG**, **LHBT** from **HLT** and **HBT** (in Arabic), as in English: "gawky" from "big" and "awkward," "muggy" from "warm" and "foggy." A dependent noun or adverb may become attached to the root: **LMS** from **LM** and **PHS** from **PH** (in Coptic). These things are common to Hamitic and Semitic.

Passing now to the Semitic languages, we find that the triliteral root has become standard. The triconsonantal pattern has taken full possession of the mind. A process of expansion is continually going on, and it is never complete. It can be illustrated in the case of nursery words, which are very primitive.

Nursery Words

Babies begin very early to make an intermittent
sound by opening and closing the lips. With the voice
sounding, this gives **ababab** or **bababa,** according to the
attention of the observer; without the voice during
closure, it gives **apapap** or **papapa;** with the voice sounding and the velum lowered it gives **amamam** or **mamama.**
A great many words in many languages have sprung
from this source: **papa, pater, father, pope, mama, mater,
mother,** and the German **amme,** to mention a few
Aryan examples. The Semites heard differently, and so
took the syllable **ab** instead of **ba** and **am** instead of **ma,**
as the basis of their words for "father" and "mother."
aB is a primitive root, containing but one consonant.
The Semitic speech-consciousness, however, sees two
consonants in it, for the vowel begins with a glottal
stop, **ʔ.** The root thus becomes **ʼB.** Hebrew lets this
be. Aramaic increases it to **ʼBB** (cf. Mark xiv. 36), or
to **ʼBH.** Arabic makes it into **ʼBH,** or **ʼBT,** or **ʼBW.**
The other primitive root, **aM,** has become everywhere
ʔMM. In the same way the primitive words **aḫ** (brother),
pū (mouth), **ḍa** (that one) have produced the longer
roots, **ʼḤW, PW** (or **ʼP**), and **ḌW** respectively.   **jad**
(hand) produces in old Arabic the root **JDJ,** and in modern
Arabic the roots **ʼJD, DJD** and **JDD.**   **dam** in modern
Arabic has the root **DMM.**

The methods by which longer roots have been produced, in the above examples, are:

(1) Recognising the glottal stop as a radical **ʼ.**
(2) Recognising the nominative ending, **-ū,** as a
    radical **W.**
(3) Prefixing a vowel and recognising the glottal
    stop as a radical **ʼ.**
(4) Prefixing the second radical.
(5) Suffixing the first radical.
(6) Suffixing the second radical.
(7) Suffixing the characterless consonant **h.**
(8) Suffixing the feminine ending **t.**

"WEAK" VERBS

Many verbs in Semitic are "weak," i.e. they are supposed to have one of the consonants ', **w,** or **j** as first, second, or third radical. These consonants in all languages are peculiar in that they serve often as "vowel-supports." In English we say "extra," "a few wextra," and "my yextra": the first with **ꜣ,** the second with **w,** and the third with **j,** according to the preceding sound. Normally a vowel will begin with **ꜣ**; but after **u(w)** it may begin with **w,** and after **i(j)** with **j.** They sometimes interchange without reason. Newsboys in New York say "wextra." Old Egyptian had a sign which stood for **ꜣ** or **j** equally. Akkadian **alādu** is the same word as Arabic **walada** and Hebrew **jālad**; and old Arabic **akala** has become **wakal** in modern Arabic. In short, ', **w,** and **j** are cognate with **a, u,** and **i.**

With the definite pattern in mind, of a word having three consonants and certain vowels, in a certain arrangement, the speaker attempts to use a root of only two consonants. He may feel that his root lacks a first radical, or a second, or a third. Where, according to his feeling, a radical has dropped out, a neighbouring vowel will expand, so as to preserve the pattern-length of the word. Where, in the course of inflection, a radical must be placed in the position of the one supposed to be lost, he will insert one of the three vowel-supports; the one suggested by the vowel in the pattern he has in mind. In Arabic the imperative is often primitive, and the perfect and imperfect often show how the root has been expanded:

Imperative.	Perfect.	Imperfect.
kul	ꜣakala	jaꜣkulu
sal	saꜣala	jasꜣalu
. . . .	qaraꜣa	jaqraꜣu
hab	wahaba	. . . .
qum	qāma	jaqūmu

Imperative.	Perfect.	Imperfect.
. . . .	ġazā	jaġzū
. . . .	jafaʻa	jaifaʻu
sir	sāra	jasīru
. . . .	ramā	jarmī

TYPICAL ELABORATIONS

Taking an imaginary root **MD**, and applying all the processes mentioned in this section and the preceding one, one might make up these roots:

MDMD	ŠMD	MDL	MDRG	ʾMD	WMD	JMD
MDD	NMD	MDB		MʾD	MWD	MJD
DMD	TMD	MDK		MDʾ	MDW	MDJ
MDM	MTD	MDH				
		MDT				

In time each of these roots might take on a special meaning, but all of them would nevertheless be developments of the original biliteral root **MD**. For a long time it has been noticed that many roots in the Hebrew or Arabic lexicon appear to possess two radicals which are more important than the third; or, in other words, that several roots are found with similar meanings, and also with two similar radicals.

SEMITIC PERFECT AND AKKADIAN PERMANSIVE

The oldest form of the so-called perfect tense of the Semitic verb[38] appears to have been:

	3.m.	3.f.	2.m.	2.f.	1.
Sg.	qatala	qatalat	qataltā	qataltī	qatalkū
Pl.	qatalū	qatalā	qataltunū	qataltinā	qatalnū

In Akkadian there is a permansive tense which would (imagining the same root to occur) give these forms:

	3.m.	3.f.	2.m.	2.f.	1.
Sg.	qatil	qatl-at	qatl-ātā	qatl-ātī	qatl-ākū
Pl.	qatl-ū	qatl-ā	qatl-ātunū	qatl-ātinā	qatl-ānī

[38] Zimmern, *Vergleichende Grammatik der Semitischen Sprachen*, 1898, p. 98.

This can hardly be called an inflection, because the endings, here set off by hyphens, may be added to any noun or adjective:

qarrad	"he is strong"
qarrad-at	"she is strong"
qarrad-ātā	"thou (masc.) art strong"
qarrad-ātī	"thou (fem.) art strong"
qarrad-ākū	"I am strong"
qarrad-ū	"they (masc.) are strong"
qarrad-ā	"they (fem.) are strong"
qarrad-ātunū	"ye (masc.) are strong"
qarrad-ātinā	"ye (fem.) are strong"
qarrad-ānī	"we are strong."

Further analysis shows that ā has by analogy crept into the endings **-ātā, -ātī, -ātunū, -ātinā, -ānī.** The resultant endings are then explained thus:

. . .	no ending, as with singular of masculine noun
-at	ending of feminine singular noun
-ū	ending of masculine plural noun
-ā	ending of feminine plural noun
-tā	shortened form of pronoun "thou," masc.
-tī	shortened form of pronoun "thou," fem.
-tunū	shortened form of pronoun "ye," masc.
-tinā	shortened form of pronoun "ye," fem.
-ākū	shortened form of pronoun "I"
-nī	shortened form of pronoun "we."

The verbal element, **qat(i)l,** then turns out to be really a nominal or adjectival element, quite as truly as **qarrad**; and the pronoun subjects are either understood, as in the third persons, or expressed by the agglutinative addition of the pronouns: at first, doubtless in their full forms, but later in abbreviated ones. **qat(i)l** is in fact a perfect participle, having a passive, active, or intransitive (qualitative) sense, and is used predicatively, though without agreeing in gender and number with its subject. It is not difficult to suppose now that the common ā of the suffixes exchanged places with the i so as to produce the forms of the Semitic perfect: qataltā, qataltunū, qataltī, qataltinā, qatalkū, and qatalnū (ū on analogy of kū). This a then replaced i in the remaining forms. and was suffixed in qatala. Or perhaps the connecting vowel ā and the end-vowel a have some other origin.

Meinhof[37] thinks that the Semitic perfect and the Akkadian permansive may originally have consisted of an uninflected verbal noun or adjective, followed by some nominal ending (e.g. the Bedauye verbal-noun ending -a, or the Somali local ending -a), followed in turn by a prefix-inflected verb "to be." With the disappearance of the root of the verb "to be," its prefixes would appear to be suffixed to the root of the principal verb. This may have happened. But the suffixes of the perfect and permansive are not the same as those of the common Semitic imperfect, and hence the postulated prefix-form would not have been identical with the imperfect that has survived in Semitic.

THE EGYPTIAN PSEUDO-PARTICIPLE

In an earlier chapter we noticed that in Egyptian and Welsh a verb with inherent subject might be made up of a crude verb form and a pronominal suffix. We need not suppose that this construction arose but once, or that every such construction in Hamitic is related directly to the Semitic perfect and permansive. In Old Egyptian[39] there was one combination which lies very near to the Semitic perfect and permansive. To the verbal root are added the endings:

	3.*m.*	3.*f.*	2.*m.*	2.*f.*	I.
Sg.	-ī	-tī	-tī	-tī	-kūī
Pl.	-ū	-ū	-tiūnī	-tiūnī	-ūin

[39] The short vowels are unknown.

Taking out the strange element **i**, which gives the combination a participial force, we have left very nearly the Semitic endings:

		Egyptian.	*Semitic.*
Sg.	3.*m.*	. . . .	. . . .
	3.*f.*	-t	-at
	2.*m.*	-t	-tā
	2.*f.*	-t	-tī
	1.	-kū	-kū
Pl.	3.*m.*	-ū	-ū
	3.*f.*	-ū	-ā
	2.*m.*	-tūnī	-tunū
	2.*f.*	-tūnī	-tinā
	1.	-ūn	-nū

SIMILAR FORMATIONS

There was another device, having in fact many variations, in which the crude verb-form was combined with another set of pronominal suffixes. Of these combinations no trace is found in Semitic. But the suffixes are interesting, because they can almost exactly be equated with the ordinary Semitic possessive pronoun suffixes.[40] Supposing the symbols[41] of the Egyptologists, **ṯ, ś,** and **f,** to stand in earlier Egyptian for the sounds **c, ç, ɸ,** and in later Egyptian for **t, s, f** (Hieroglyphic orthography and the Coptic forms indicate that they do), we may thus equate the two sets of suffixes:

		Egyptian Suffixes	*Value in Mid. Emp.*	*Value in Old Emp.*	*Supposed Links*	*Old Semitic*	*Supposed Oldest Semitic*
Sg.	3.*m.*	-f	-f	-f	-ɸ -ɸu	-hū	-sū
	3.*f.*	-ś	-s	-ç	-çi	-hī[42]	-sī
	2.*m.*	-k	-k	-k	-ka	-kā	-kā
	2.*f.*	-ṯ	-t	-c	-ci	-kī	-kī
	1.	-j	-i	-i	-i	-ī	-aja

[40] See note 29.   [41] See list of symbols.

	Egyptian Suffixes	Value in Mid. Emp.	Value in Old Emp.	Supposed Links		Old Semitic	Supposed Oldest Semitic
Pl. 3.m.						-hunū	-sunū
	-śn	-sn	-çn	-çin	-hin		
3.f.						-hinā	-sinā
2.m.						-kunū	-kunū
	-ṭn	-tn	-cn	-cin	-kin		
2.f.						-kinā	-kinā
1.	-n	-n	-n	-na		-nā	-nā

Here there is plainly a direct relationship. But the
Egyptian forms are much changed from their originals
by the operation of labialisation and palatalisation.
The rounding of the lips for **u** has changed **h** into **φ** and
then **f**. The raising of the front of the tongue for **i** has
changed **h** into **ç** and **k** into **c**. This happened before
Egyptian came to be written down at all; and by the
end of the Old Empire the resulting sounds had again
changed, breaking down into simpler articulations.
Labialisation and palatalisation occur in different
language-families, and are particularly characteristic
of some. The Egyptian forms are derivable from old,
but not the oldest, Semitic ones.

THE IMPERFECT OF THE VERB

The oldest form of the so-called imperfect tense of
the Semitic verb[43] appears to have been:

	3.m.	3.f.	2.m.	2.f.	1.
Sg.	ja-qtul	ta-qtul	ta-qtul	ta-qtul-ī	a-qtul
Pl.	ja-qtul-ū	ja-qtul-ā	ta-qtul-ū	ta-qtul-ā	na-qtul

The prefixes here are not the same as those used with
the perfect and the permansive. The feminines are
given the inferiority-sign, **t,** to distinguish them from

---

[42] **hī** is the independent, not the suffix, form in the languages having **h**;
but Akkadian has the corresponding form, **šī**, with verbs.

[43] Zimmern, *op. cit.*, p. 105.

the corresponding masculines; and the second persons are given the same inferiority-sign to distinguish them from the first persons, in accordance with the old dichotomy. Plurals are given the old noun-endings, -ū (masc.) and -ā (fem.), which have figured in the preceding tables. The second person feminine singular, belonging to both inferior classes at once, receives the old feminine suffix -ī. The third person feminine plural, having the feminine plural ending -ā, does not require the t in its prefix.

Egyptian shows no trace of the imperfect. But Agau, a Cushitic Hamitic language, has a prefix-verbal form in which "she" is distinguished from "he" and "you" from "I" by the inferiority-sign t, while the two superiors, "he" and "I" fall together. In Bedauye and Somali even the last two are distinguished, as in Semitic; and the prefixes are the same or similar. The Somali imperfect is constructed thus:

	3.*m.*	3.*f.*	2.*m.*	2.*f.*	1.
Sg.	ji-mād-a	ti-mād-a	ti-mād-a	ti-mād-a	i-mād-a
Pl.	ji-mād-ān	ti-mād-ān	ti-mād-ān	ti-mād-ān	ni-mād-a

-a is here the sign of past time; and -ān is this a plus a common plural ending -an. The second person feminine singular is not especially distinguished; all the prefixes have an i- vowel instead of the a of Semitic. Otherwise the Somali inflection is the same.

A SIMILAR FORMATION

In the Hausa language there exists a prefix-conjugation consisting simply of the regular pronouns and a verbal stem:

	3.*m.*	3.*f.*	2.*m.*	2.*f.*	1.
Sg.	ja-so	ta-so	ka-so	ki-so	ni-so
Pl.	su-so	su-so	ku-so	ku-so	mu-so

Instead of the **t** of inferiority in the second persons the ordinary pronouns are used. These pronouns, though used as subjects, are the pronouns which Semitic uses as objects:

		Hausa.	*Supposed oldest Semitic.*
Sg.	2.*m.*	**ka-**	**-kā**
	2.*f.*	**ki-**	**-kī**
Pl.	2.*m.*	**ku-**	**-kunū**
	2.*f.*	**ku-**	**-kinā**

The Hausa pronoun **ki-** is made up of **ka-** and the old feminine suffix **-ī**, and **ku-** is made up of **ka-** and the old plural masculine suffix **-ū**. (The Semitic suffixes may be interrelated in much the same way.) Gender distinction is lost in both the second and the third persons of the plural, so that **su-** stands for supposed Old Semitic object-pronouns **-sunū** and **-sinā**. In the first persons, **ni-** corresponds to the Semitic object-pronoun **-nī**; and **mu-**, which consists of **ni-** and the old plural masculine suffix **-ū**, (through an intermediate form **nu-**), corresponds to the Semitic object pronoun **-nā** or **-nū**. **ja-,** so widespread in Hamitic and Semitic, here finds an explanation. It is the ordinary Hausa pronoun for the third person singular masculine.

This Hausa prefix-conjugation has only two forms, **ja-so** and **ta-so** identical with the Semitic imperfect; and only one, **ta-so,** using the inferiority-sign which is the essence of the Semitic imperfect. The Hausa conjugation therefore is not a form of the imperfect found in Semitic and Somali. It is a similar prefix-formation, using chiefly the pronouns instead of the inferiority-sign **t.**

We may now explain all the prefixes and suffixes of the regular Hamitic-Semitic imperfect thus: (1) **ja-** is the pronoun "he." (2) **na-** is the pronoun "we." (3) **a-** is the naked vowel derived from **ja** and **na-**, and indicating really no pronoun at all. (4) **ta-** is this vowel, **a,** preceded by the inferiority-sign, **t,** and

indicating "she" and "you." (5) **-ī** is a feminine suffix
which, in conjunction with **ta-,** means "you, woman."
(6) **-ū** is a masculine plural suffix which, in conjunction
with **ja-,** means "they," and with **ta-,** "ye, men."
(7) **-ā** is a feminine plural suffix which, in conjunction
with **ja-,** means "ye, women."

Lost Tense Distinctions

In most Semitic languages there are but two "tenses,"
a perfect and an imperfect. The perfect generally
expresses completed action, and the imperfect, uncompleted action, but often the reverse. In Akkadian
the imperfect form splits into two varieties, **iqtul** and
iqatal, the former signifying completed and the latter
uncompleted action, while the analogue of the perfect
expresses condition resulting from action. This is an
older state of affairs. In Hamitic the suffix-conjuga-
tions, corresponding to the Semitic perfect, and the
prefix-conjugations, corresponding to the Semitic imperfect, are not in any sense complementary, but quite
independent formations. Both of them can be made to
distinguish complete and incomplete action by variation
of their vowels. This ancient system fell into disuse
in Semitic; but the vowel distinctions persisted, and to
some extent assumed new functions, as organs may do
in living bodies. So we find in Arabic, e.g. verbs of
the forms, **qatala/jaqtulu, ǧalasa/jaǧlisu, qataʿa/jaqtaʿu,**
signifying action; verbs of the forms **salima/jaslamu,**
signifying temporary condition; verbs of the form
zarufa/jazrufu, signifying inherent quality. But even
these distinctions have fallen into some confusion.

Conclusion

Although comparative Hamitic-Semitic studies are
not yet upon a satisfactory foundation, it is difficult,
after examining the known facts, to deny that Hamitic
and Semitic are fundamentally related, and that
Hamitic represents the survival of conditions more
primitive than those to be found in Semitic.

CHAPTER V.

Hamites

LOOKING at a language-map of Africa we see that Semitic is current: (1) To the north, west, and east, of the Sahara, where it has been introduced by the Moslem Arabs since the seventh century A.D.; (2) in Abyssinia and that region, where it was probably brought from South Arabia sometime before the Christian Era. The first, Arabic, is not African; nor probably the second, Ge'ez (Ethiopic), with its many modern relatives. The racial type of these speakers of Semitic indicates that they have absorbed a Hamitic population, already more or less nigridised; only in the eastern Sudan have they been superimposed directly upon Negro stock. With that exception, then, all the Semitic territory was formerly Hamitic. Having eliminated the Semites, we see that there remain five linguistic stocks: (1) Hamitic, (2) Hottentot, (3) Bantu, (4) Sudanic, and (5) Bushman. Of these, Hottentot is now held to be a fusion of Hamitic and Bushman, and Bantu a fusion of Sudanic and proto-Hamitic. There remain then only three native and distinct African language-families, and these three correspond to the three basic African races[44]: (1) Hamites, (2) True Negroes, (3) Bushmen.

What the original position of these three was upon the African continent we can only infer from their present position. Hamites apparently once occupied the Sahara, true Negroes or Sudanians the Sudan and equatorial Africa, with Bushmen further south. With each glaciation of Europe the crowding population of the

[44] Leaving the Pygmies out of account.

G

then fruitful Sahara must have pressed hard against the Negroes to the south, penetrating far into equatorial Africa and even reaching the Cape. With the recession of the ice in Europe the Sahara dried up gradually and, becoming less hospitable, was abandoned in its more arid portions to the Negroes.

DISTRIBUTION OF HAMITES

In the larger sense "Hamitic" may be applied to the Mediterranean White race, on both shores of the Mediterranean. In a narrower sense the name applies to the African division of that race, separated from the European by the disappearance of the land-bridges across the western Mediterranean. These African Hamites probably once occupied the northernmost third of Africa, including what is now the Sahara and the coastal lands. With the gradual desiccation of the east-central Sahara they became divided, as we have seen. Some migrated southward into the western Sudan. Their descendants are decidedly Negroid, and speak very primitive (Hausa) or proto-Hamitic (Ful) tongues. Others survived along the coast (Shilh, Kabyle) and even within the western Sahara (Tuareg). Their descendants are the fairest and most like Europeans, and speak languages of the Libyan type. Still others settled in the more moist lands about the eastern Horn of Africa. Their descendants are more or less Negroid, and speak languages of the Cushitic type. (Bedauye, Somali, and many others), most closely related to Semitic. In the lake region they were nearly absorbed by the Negroes, and in the far south, by the Bushmen.

EASTERN HAMITES

Our interest must now be directed to the Hamitic groups which produced the Egyptians. They are the Cushitic and the Libyan.

From earliest times the Nile valley must have been inhabited. With the repeated drying up of the Sahara

BEDAUYE WOMAN.

OLD EGYPTIAN TYPE.

Peasant from Upper Egypt, near Assiut, with light brown
skin, straight brown hair, lips and nose of the old Pharaonic
type.

OLD EGYPTIAN TYPE.

Ti, a royal architect and pyramid-builder of 2700 B.C., from
a portrait-statue in the Cairo Museum.

OLD EGYPTIAN TYPE.

A scribe of the Old Empire, from a portrait-statue in the Cairo Museum.

it must have served as a refuge for a few of the strongest
of eastern Hamites. In the course of time the valley-
dwellers must have developed a special type of physique,
of speech, and of culture. They were, of course, allied
to the near-by Cushitic Hamites, but not identical with
them. They were probably much like the present-day
Bedauye, a wild pastoral folk who live in the deserts east
of the Nile, but formerly inhabited the valley between
Assuan and Wadi Halfa. The valley Egyptians became
a mighty people, with a culture of their own, though
not of high degree.

Quite distinct from Upper Egypt, the Valley, was
Lower Egypt, the Delta. It was an appendix to
Egypt proper, marshy and undefended, from the very
beginning of history invaded and occupied by Hamitic
nomads of the Sahara. These were Libyans, like the
modern Tuareg or the Berbers of the Atlas, having less
Negro blood than the Valley Egyptians. They differed
also in speech and culture from the Valley people whose
affinities were Cushitic.

Cushitic-Libyan Mixture

Egyptian civilisation received a great impetus when,
at about 3300 B.C., Menes, a king of Upper Egypt,
conquered (?) the Delta people and united the crowns
of Upper and Lower Egypt. Within four hundred
years began a period of progress in the command of
mechanical appliances and the organisation and control
of men unparalleled in history until modern times.
From the earliest stone masonry (B.C. 3050) to the
Great Pyramid (begun B.C. 2900) there was an interval
of only a hundred and fifty years. Nothing of the kind
was ever seen again in Egypt. It was like the impetus
given to civilisation in Greece when invaded by the
Hellenic barbarians from the European north. In the
case of Egypt a somewhat nigridised Mediterranean
race was infused with purer Mediterranean blood. In
the case of Greece it was Mediterranean infused with

Nordic. In both cases a sedentary people was enlivened by the addition of highly selected immigrant nomad stock. Perhaps in both cases the mixture was biologically fortunate. In both cases there seems then to have ensued a decline of ability, as though the enlivening foreign ingredient were being slowly eliminated by climate and other conditions of life unsuited to it.

LIBYANS IN EGYPT

Libyans are mentioned in Egyptian records from earliest times as turbulent nomads upon the western border, in the oases and the Delta. During the nineteenth and twentieth dynasties (1350–1090 B.C.) they threatened Egypt with a devastating invasion. As early as 1100 B.C. they were employed in the Egyptian army as mercenaries, and later as leaders, with the result that they reached the throne of the Pharoahs in the twenty-second dynasty (945–745 B.C.).

The names applied to them by the Egyptians are:[45]

(1) **THNW,** on the northern part of the western frontier; (2) **TMHW,** on the southern part of the western frontier; (3) **RBW,** near Cyrenaica; (4) **MŠWŠ,** west of the **RBW.** Besides these, a number of tribal names.

As Egyptian writing used its r-sign for the l-sound when necessary, **RBW** may quite as well be read **LBW,** yielding the name under which all North Africans were known to the Hebrews, Greeks and Romans: **Lūbīm (Lehābīm), Libyes, Libyi**—the English "Libyans."

MŠWŠ, which lacks the plural ending and must be a collective noun, has been equated by Bates with the root **MZĠ,** meaning "noble" or "free," and is found in various modern Hamitic tribal names: **Imushagh, Imazighen, Imaziren, Imagighen, Tamaseght,** as well as in ancient classical forms: **Mazices, Masages, Mazyes, Maxyes.**

---

[45] The **W** in each case is the plural ending and not a part of the root. For these names see Bates, *The Eastern Libyans,* 1914, pp. 46 ff.

The twenty-third and twenty-fourth dynasties (745–712 B.C.) reigned in Tanis, a city of the Delta; and the twenty-sixth dynasty (663–525 B.C.) in Sais, also a city of the Delta, and in particular the place where **NT** (Neit), the ancient goddess of Lower Egypt, was worshipped. Neit was the goddess of the Libyan people, goddess of hunting and weaving, the two nomadic arts. She was worshipped in the earliest dynasties, and now in the twenty-sixth she became the state-divinity. The Delta seems to have been Libyan from the beginning, and to have remained so down to the Persian period.

Negroes in Egypt

In the Osiris legend, which unfortunately has reached us in a late redaction, the god is murdered by his brother, Set. Isis, his wife and sister brings his body to Egypt. Set scatters his dismembered body. Isis then seeks and collects the fragments, erecting shrines in the places where they are found. Thereupon Isis, with Horus, her son, attacks Set and drives him out of Egypt.

An inscription upon the Temple of Edfu states, according to Petrie,[46] that the struggle of Osiris and Set was a tribal war in which the people of Set were conquered and driven out. Osiris was worshipped all over Egypt in prehistoric times. Isis was a divinity of the Delta, and Horus of Upper Egypt. All were human figures. But Set was an animal-headed god. Perhaps the rivalry was between Hamitic worshippers of human gods, and Negro worshippers of animal-gods.

Animal-Gods

The most surprising element in Egyptian religion is the worship of animal-headed gods, animal-gods, and actual living animals. In a people of such intelligence and ability as the Egyptians this demands an explanation.

[46] *The Religion of Ancient Egypt*, p. 39 ff.

Some think that the animal-gods are late degenerations of a primitive symbolism. The baboon is the emblem of wisdom, the lion of destruction, the bull and ram of reproduction, the hippopotamus of pregnancy, the vulture of maternity, the jackal of lonely places. Some, but not all, of these became actual gods; notably the bull of Memphis and the Ram of Thebes.

It is easier to believe that the animal-gods were at first observed, and feared or reverenced, because of their resemblance to human beings, or their possession of human traits. The habit of mimicry and interest in mimicry is Negro, and the mental habit of regarding animals as brethren is notoriously Negro also. Totemism is, of course, common to many parts of the world, but animal-stories are chiefly found among Negroes. The "Uncle Remus" tales of the Southern States of America are good examples. It is this element which has given the Abyssinian Semites their lively interest in animals and animal-stories. In India the trait is probably Dravidian, and has something to do with the origins of Hindu belief in metempsychosis.

In the course of time the animal-gods became humanised, retaining the animal-head by way of symbolism. Later they may have been held by individuals to be mere symbols of abstract qualities. But their origin appears to have been a very humble one, and points to a Negro strain in the Egyptian people.

PERMANENCY OF EGYPTIAN TYPE

The climate of Egypt is hot, but apparently not hostile to individuals. Invalids from Europe find it favourable to their comfort and recovery. And yet Europeans are unable to bring up their children there. Probably the British suffer more than Italians and Greeks; but even the Greeks do not maintain themselves indefinitely. For some three hundred years before and after the beginning of the Christian era there were many

Greeks in Egypt; and yet no Greek strain can be detected in the modern Egyptian. It is so with plants and domestic animals. The water-buffalo and the ass thrive, but not the cow and the horse. European trees cannot be maintained in the Ezbekiyah Gardens of Cairo. Grapes will grow only in the Fayyūm. It is not surprising then to find a very definite human type in Egypt, and one which has not changed from remotest times to the present. When an ancient wooden portrait-statue was uncovered the workmen thought it represented their village chieftain, and called it the "Sheich el-Beled."

Peasant and Pharaonic Types

Two types are distinguishable in ancient and modern Egypt. The one is broad-faced, with high cheek bones; the other, narrow-faced, with convex nose and full, though not Negroid, lips. The first is exemplified by Khephren, the royal architect, and the scribe;[47] it seems to have been the common type in antiquity, and is the common peasant type to-day. The second is illustrated by Rameses II,[48] and our peasant from Upper Egypt;[49] it is the type which one thinks of as an Egyptian face, and is rare among the modern inhabitants of the country. The first is found among the Somali, and the second among the Hima, as pictured by Meinhof and von Luschan.[50] Possibly the peasant type represents the stock of the old Valley Egyptians, and the Pharaonic type, the purer Libyan strain of the Delta.

The Egyptian Mind

Curiousity, keen perception, ingenuity, and great skill of hand, were joined to conservatism, conventionality, and a religious outlook. The accuracy of their portrait-statues cannot be doubted, and convinces us that, had they wished to do so, they might have left

[47] In the Cairo Museum. The last two here illustrated.
[48] In the Turin Museum.   [49] Here illustrated.
[50] *Die Sprachen der Hamiten*, Plates III, VI.

us realistic drawings, with depth and perspective, and statues equal to those of the Greeks. In everything they did they showed accuracy and care, a love of nicety, and a sense of beauty. How favourably do Egyptian figures compare with the squat and shapeless sculptures of the Hittites and even the Babylonians, inferior in taste and workmanship, often hideous in their conception. There was in Egypt both joy of life and consciousness of life unending; poetic insight, and moral perception. The Sumerians and Akkadians were devoted to commerce and shamanism in this world, and entertained but dim and disheartening ideas of a future state. As early as 3000 B.C. the Egyptians had invented an alphabet of twenty-four letters. They predicted astronomical phenomena. They treated diseases. But the arts and sciences were regarded as fixed from the beginning, when they were received complete from the hand of the god Thoth. In art they dared not depart from ancient standards, which they could not have failed to know were false. In writing they dared not discard the ancient accumulation of idiograms, determinatives, and root signs down to the very end of paganism. In science they were unable to classify, interpret, and co-ordinate their observations. Their astronomy became lost in astrology, and their medicine in magic. They did not trust their minds, and they walked in the trodden paths.

BEGINNINGS OF CIVILISATION

The temperate zones are most favourable to a high degree of civilisation; but it is difficult to withstand their winters without a rather elaborate material equipment. Without this there is little leisure for invention and discovery. It is natural then that civilisation should begin in warmer lands, and gradually extend to colder ones, there to reach its highest perfection. Down to 3000 B.C. the European Nordics, Mediterraneans and Alpines were still without the art of writing and

without metals. At about that time civilisation appears
in two highly favoured spots; the valley of the Nile,
and the alluvial plain of the Tigris and Euphrates;
in the first instance among Mediterranean Whites, and
in the second among Mongoloids (?). Negroes have
never originated a civilisation nor successfully borrowed
one, although not altogether confined to very hot
regions, and although in contact with highly progressive
peoples since early times. We may suppose that a
sudden advance in the art of living came in Egypt and
Babylonia because of a favourable conjunction of race
and environment. But this does not explain it all. A
series of happy circumstances may have given certain
communities an initial advantage after which successes
came by leaps and bounds.

EGYPTIAN CIVILISATION

We have seen that the higher Egyptian civilisation
began where Valley and Delta meet, and made its way
up-stream; that, after a brief archaic period, it speedily
reached its culmination; and that it contained two
distinct elements.

The Egyptian religion in particular shows diversity of
origin and complete indifference to consistency; for
the Egyptians were conservative and unco-ordinative.
Some of the gods were animal or animal-headed, others
were human, others were cosmic, others abstract; a
few were of foreign origin. The dead man was supposed
to be consciously resident at his grave, as the Upper
Egyptian peasant still imagines him to be, in spite of
official Islam. This is probably the belief of the oldest
inhabitants of the Nile valley, who buried their dead
with food and drink. But according to the ancient
Osirian faith the soul went to judgment in another
world. The soul declared its innocence of the "forty-
two sins"; the heart was weighed against an ostrich
feather; and the deceased, if his heart was "light,"
went to the heavenly fields, there to live in bliss, after

the manner of the best in this world. At the same time the soul was supposed to sail away on a heavenly barque to the setting sun, there to dwell with the blessed, occupied in repelling the powers of darkness by magic spells. This did not prevent the elaborate preparation of the mummy, as though against a day of resurrection in the flesh upon this earth. A man had not only a body, a soul (personality and passions), and a spirit (animating principle), but also a "ba" (the cemetery owl), a "shadow," and a "name." The three last are common in superstition the world over, and particularly in the East. Owls are human-faced birds which haunt graveyards at night and utter strange and mournful cries. A man's shadow is his living, moving double, following him everywhere, expanding with his morning strength, and shrinking with his noonday faintness. A man's name is his sacred self, and careless or malevolent use of it will injure him. Perhaps Egyptian religion was not more diverse in origin than other national pagan systems, but the Egyptian people were less inclined to system.

Religious Consciousness

The purpose of religious rites and practices was to secure the favour of the gods. There was no wish for pardon because there was no "consciousness of sin." If one's heart proved after death to be weighted down with the forty-two sins, then there was no help, no repentance, no redemption: as though the whole matter were beyond one's power to control. This did not, however, prevent a lively sense of obligation in the conduct of life in this world. It must not be thought that this strange people who spent so much time and labour upon preparations for death, were on that account lugubrious. They were, on the contrary, a joyous and happy people, who in life took all that life could offer, in order that in death the soul might not regret having missed any of its allotted satisfactions.

Peculiarly Hamitic Traits

Egyptian traits which strike us as peculiar and which at the same time are said to be found more or less among other Hamites are: (1) Independence and equality of women, (2) marriage of brother and sister, (3) circumcision, (4) mummification, (5) pork tabu, (6) cult of the cat, (7) erection of megaliths.

Women in ancient Egypt occupied a high social position, and were equal to men before the law. They had the right of independent domicile, and might initiate divorce proceedings. We are reminded of Tuareg women who have successfully opposed the polygamy of Islam and who are the custodians of Tuareg literary tradition. With this status and freedom goes a certain indifference to the relations of the sexes— whether as cause or as result. Even in Christian Egypt marriage was a private arrangement rather than a religious mystery. The Christian Abyssinians, who are partly Hamitic in race and traditions, allow themselves great freedom in this matter.

Perhaps the marriage of brothers and sisters is one manifestation of indifference toward the relations of the sexes. Some of the Pharaohs married their sisters in order to keep the royal blood pure. Lesser persons did the same to avoid division of agricultural lands. There was always the divine sanction of the Osirian precedent. Such a practice is hard to parallel anywhere, and its reported occurrence among the Guanches is remarkable if true.

With the other characteristic there is more difficulty in making out a case. Circumcision occurs among Hamites and non-Hamites. In Egypt it was a very ancient custom, though perhaps not religious, or general, or obligatory. The Guanches did not practice it. Mummification of dead bodies is attested of the Guanches, and of the Egyptians after the first few dynasties, but of no other Hamites. Yet it was practiced in Peru. Tabu of the swine is common, though not universal, among Hamites, and is found among other races. The cult of the cat did not appear in Egypt before about 2000 b.c., and is explained by the fact that the animal originated in Nubia and became indispensable to the inhabitants of the rat-infested valley of the Nile. The supposedly Malayan Hovas of Madagascar display a reverence for the cat that is perhaps the only parallel to old Egyptian fanaticism; but nothing of the kind is observed among other Hamites. The Egyptian obelisks and Abyssinian monoliths remind one of Stonehenge and certain Neolithic monuments in France, but also of entirely independent structures in Central America. The dolmens, cromlechs, and menhirs of Europe and northern Africa are not large enough in most cases to be seriously considered.

Egyptian Writing

Analysis of speech into its component sounds is by no means an easy task, even after the idea of doing so has occurred to one. The representation of sounds by written symbols is a conception bold beyond the power of imagination. Speech is, for the natural man, as concrete a thing as consciousness; and there is no natural connection between a thing written and a thing heard. Egyptians invented the first true alphabet at the very beginning of their history. They hit upon it by a process which has occurred elsewhere.

(1) In the mind there is a connection between the visual image of a thing, the idea of the thing, and the kinesthetic-auditory image of the word signifying that thing. A knife held up to view brings the idea of "knife" to the mind of every beholder; the sound of the word "knife" echoes in his ear; he unconsciously frames the word "knife" with his speech-organs, and feels the sensation of his saying "knife."

(2) A picture of the knife will do as well as the actual article. This is the stage of Amerind writing.

(3) The picture may acquire a fixed and conventional connection with some one word of the language, to the exclusion of synonyms or words expressing related ideas. This is the idiographic stage.

(4) The picture comes to stand for the sounds of the word, not primarily for its sense. As Egyptian was a Hamitic language in which, as in Semitic, the root-idea resided in a framework of consonants, the picture came to stand for one or more consonants, without any reference to the vowels of the word as actually pronounced.

Akkadian had a different development at this point. It had taken over its cuneiform system from the Sumerians, who spoke a language of the monosyllabic type in which consonants and vowels had equal weight. The signs therefore had come to stand for short syllables containing both consonants and vowels, whereas the Egyptian came to stand for roots containing consonants only. Akkadian was a Semitic language and therefore of the same type as Egyptian. The old Sumerian writing was ill adapted to such languages, although it has the advantage for us of representing the vowels.

(5) The picture is used for some other word having the same consonants as the original one. It is now possible to represent words for abstract ideas, of which there can be no picture or visual image, in the manner of a rebus. Foreign names, which have no meaning in the language, can also be represented.

(6) Pictures representing certain short words are used to represent the consonants of syllables frequently recurring in the process of building up verb and other word-forms. This is the syllabic stage.

(7) Phonetic analysis of the language leads to determination of all the consonants occurring in it. Pictures representing short words come to stand for a single consonant contained in the word.

Instead of using this excellent alphabet, the Egyptians

elaborated combinations of idiograms with deter-
minative, syllabic, and alphabetic signs, in fixed combinations which had to be memorised. To complicate
matters still more, the beautifully pictorial old Hieroglyphic style gave place to an every-day hand, Hieratic,
and this again to an abbreviated script, Demotic. All
this was swept away by Christianity, which brought
with it the simple Greek alphabet in which the Egyptian
language at last appeared under the name of "Coptic."

THE EGYPTIAN LANGUAGE

The Egyptian language can be followed from about
3000 B.C. to about 1500 A.D., when its last echoes were
heard by occasional travellers in remote villages of
Upper Egypt. The Coptic of Christian Egypt is
separated from the classical language of the Middle
Empire by about 2000 years, and from the language of
the Old Empire by about 3000 years. During this long
career of 4500 years it passed through three phases,
amounting to distinct languages, without losing its
agglutinative character, as other Hamitic languages have
done. As fast as the old agglutinative combinations
fused into inflections, new agglutinations were built
up. Thus in Old Egyptian the sentence "The god has
heard thy voice," would be:

śḏm nṯr ḥrw-k, "Hearing-of-god voice-of-thee";
while in Coptic:

a-f-sōtm ntši p-noute m-pe-k-hroou = "Did-he-hearing
namely-the-god namely-the-of-thee-voice."

EGYPTIAN SOUNDS

The vowels of Egyptian are unknown except as they
appear in Coptic. Of the consonants represented in the
oldest form of the language only, **q, ʾ, ʿ,** and **ḫ** are
Hamitic-Semitic. There are no "emphatic" consonants, unless possibly **q**; but the "pressure-articulation"
is represented by **ʿ** and **ḫ.** Palatalisation has produced

the unfamiliar sounds ʝ, c, and ç. There is also a new
ch-sound which possibly may have the value ʁ.

The complete list of consonants would then be:

	Labials.	Dentals.	Palatals.	Velars.	Uvulars.	Laryngals.
Stops	b	d	ʝ	g		
	p	t	c	k	q	ʔ
Fricatives	w		j			ꞓ
	f	s ʃ	ç	x	ʁ	h ḥ
Vibrants.		r				
Nasals	m	n				

CHAPTER VI.

Semites

ORIGIN

THE previous chapters were intended to show that the Semitic peoples have all migrated from Arabia, and that they are related to the Hamitic peoples in Africa, and to the Mediterranean branch of the White race in Europe.

EARLIER AND LATER PHASES

Cross-correspondencies between the different Semitic languages are such that Akkadian and South Arabic (with Abyssinian) must be regarded as older phases of Semitic speech in general, while all the others, Canaanitish, Aramaean, and Arabic (North Arabic) must be regarded as sprung from a later phase.[51] The peculiarities of the older phase are:

(1) Causative prefix and personal pronoun of the third person have the **s** and **š** instead of **h** and **'**.

(2) First person singular of the perfect ends in **-ku,** not **-tu.**

(3) Imperfect has two forms, with tense-functions (Akkadian) or mood-functions (Ethiopic).

(4) Prefixes of derived stems may be combined more freely.

(5) Older vocabulary.

---

[51] Christian, *Akkader und Südaraber als ältere Semitenschicht*, in *Anthropos,* 1922, XIV–XV, pp. 729 ff.

North and South Semitic

Independently of the division into earlier and later,
the Semitic languages may be classified as northern and
southern. To the first belong Akkadian, Canaanitish,
and Aramaean; to the second, Arabic and South Arabic
(with Ethiopic and other Abyssinian Semitic languages).
The mark of southern Semitic is the so-called "broken
plural."

Broken Plurals

We have had occasion several times to speak of
certain abstract or collective nouns, treated by grammar
as feminine singulars, but usurping the function of
plurals, in all the South Semitic tongues. Such abstracts and collectives are found nearly everywhere.
In English we say "youth" or "manhood" in place of
"youths" and "men." But it is most unusual to allow
them to take the place of regular plural forms. It is
the fact that they remain true feminine singulars that
is remarkable, and that they occur in such great numbers.
They are called "broken" by the Arab grammarians
because the singular form appears to have been completely broken up and made over into the plural. To
us they appear, in all but a very few cases, not to have
been derived at all from the singular, but to be independent formations, selected because of some contrast
which they present when associated with the singular.
This is of course a case of the dichotomy which has been
noticed in Hamitic. It has been suggested that certain
forms may have arisen through reduplication of the
singular or some part of it, and this may be true of a
very few cases. In general they are vowel-and-
consonant patterns in the mind, into which words seem
to flow without any apparent reason. So the French
words "journal" and "hotel" are unhesitatingly made
into the plurals **ǧarānīl** and **hawātīl** by the modern
speaker of Arabic.

H

One sort of broken plural does seem to contain a
definite sign in the shape of an **a** between the second
and third radicals:

	Arabic.	Ethiopic.	Hausa.
Sg.	ḥalq-atun	ᵓegr	
Pl.	ḥalaq-un	ᵓegar	
Sg.	qiṣṣ-atun	mesl	
Pl.	qiṣaṣ-un	mesal	
Sg.	ʿulb-atun	ᵓezn	murfu
Pl.	ʿulab-un	ᵓezan	murafu

In northern Semitic there seems to be a trace of this
device. But it is never employed except in conjunction
with the regular plural endings. It does not produce a
feminine singular, but a regular plural.

	Hebrew.	Syriac (pre-classical).
Sg.	melek (originally **malk**)	amm-ā
Pl.	melāk-īm (originally **melak-īm**)	amam-ē
Sg.	sēfer (originally **sifr**)	
Pl.	sefār-īm (originally **sefar-īm**)	
Sg.	bōqer (originally **buqr**)	
Pl.	beqār-īm (originally **beqar-īm**)	

Syriac in a very few cases uses abstracts or collectives
in place of plurals: ḥemr-ā as plural of ḥmār-ā. But
they are rare, and in most cases bear the regular plural
ending: ṭalāj-ē as plural of ṭalj-ā. They are not treated
as feminine singulars, but as plurals.

Reduplication of the whole or of a part of the singular
to form the plural, occurs in North Semitic. The
Hebrew word **majim** and **šāmajim** are plurals without
singulars, seeming to have the dual ending **-ajim,** but
in reality going back to the forms **maimai** and
šamaimai. Akkadian has **alkak-ātū** (for **alk-ātu**) from
the singular **alak-tu,** and perhaps **abbū** from **abu** and
aḫḫu from **aḫu.** But these are rare and in some cases

very doubtful, often using the regular plural ending, and always considered as a plural, not a feminine singular abstract or collective.

We may say then with confidence that North Semitic has lost all consciousness of the broken plural as an institution. Very rarely it may use an abstract for a plural, as we may do in English. Reduplicated forms occur, as in other languages, but they have the plural ending and are true plurals. Only in nouns like **melek, sēfer, bōqer,** is there a trace of the true broken plural of the south. The meaning of the inserted **-a-** has been forgotten, and the plural endings are added.

Hamitic not only has broken plurals of reduplication, and those with inserted **-a-,** but the kind which depends upon a contrast of long vowels between singular and plural:

	Bedauye.	*Arabic.*
Sg.	dōf	šarīf
Pl.	dāf	širāf
Sg.	genūf	ḥimār
Pl.	genīf	ḥamīr

Egyptian, to judge from its last stage, Coptic, possessed plural forms (not abstracts or collectives, singular) with vowel changes like those in certain well-known broken-plural formations; but they are explained by some as the result of sound-changes.

Old South Semitic, represented by South Arabic and Ethiopic, has definitely gone over to the use of broken plurals; but they have fewer forms than in Arabic.

From the foregoing we may conclude that the broken plural: (1) began, with a restricted number of forms and a limited application, in old Hamito-Semitic, (2) existed in the earliest Semitic speech, (3) increased its forms and range of application somewhat in primitive South Semitic, and still more in later South Semitic, (4) was lost in even the most primitive North Semitic, except for a few traces in certain plural forms.

ANTIQUITY OF SEPARATION

We meet with the various North Semitic languages in each case not long after they have been brought out of the desert by the great migrations. Such a fundamental thing as the broken plural could not possibly be lost independently by several languages in so short a time. North Semitic therefore must have been brought from some common centre in which the broken plural did not exist, and South Semitic from a centre where it was highly developed. The two centres must have been peopled by primitive Semites at a time when the broken plural had suffered neither atrophy nor hypertrophy; and they must then have been isolated from each other for a long time. The Najd may have been the North Semitic, and Yemen the South Semitic centre.

GREAT SEMITIC MIGRATIONS

Arabia is an unfruitful land. Its people are prolific. They are at all times near to distress. Even in better times, over-population exerts a pressure from within, and its people leave the country quietly along the routes of travel and trade. But there have been crises, climatic, or economic, or political, when the peninsula poured out its surplus in an inundating flood. Such migrations appear to have occurred as early as 3500 B.C., and at intervals, roughly, of a thousand years thereafter. The first brought into Babylonia its oldest Semitic stock; the second, the Canaanites into Palestine and the second wave of Semites into Babylonia; the third, the Aramaean or Syrian peoples; the fourth, the Nabataeans, the fifth, the Arabs. Perhaps the third and fifth were the greatest. In the first migration came a more primitive type of Semitic speech, which with the second migration had changed to the common one. With the fourth migration came people who spoke, not the North Semitic of previous waves, but South Semitic with its broken plurals. Perhaps we may believe that between

the first and second migrations a later type of speech
had taken possession of central Arabia, as Christian
thinks;[51] and that between the third and fourth the
speech of the South Semitic centre had moved up into
the old centre of North Semitic.

SEMITIC PEOPLES

For our purposes the important Semitic groups are:
(1) Babylonians (including Assyrians and Chaldaeans),
(2) Canaanites (including Phoenicians), (3) Hebrews
(including Aramaeans). Other important groups are:
(4) South Arabians (including Abyssinians), (5) Nabataeans, (6) Arabs. Of the last three the Old Testament
is only vaguely aware, or entirely ignorant. The first
three then will concern us primarily; and the last three
will be considered only incidentally.

PHYSICAL TYPES

When we speak of "Semites" we mean, of course,
speakers of Semitic languages and, by implication,
peoples inheriting in some degree the blood of that
ancient White community in Arabia in whose midst
the Semitic type of speech developed.

But the Semitic-speaking hordes from Arabia found
in the Fertile Crescent ancient settled populations of
very complex make-up; and the historically known
Semitic peoples of this region are merely ancient
populations, freshly infused with Semitic blood, and
speaking the Semitic language brought in by their most
recent Semitic conquerors. So, we find the Babylonians
and Assyrians strongly marked in appearance by some
racial influence encountered by them after leaving the
desert, and perpetuated by the Nestorian Christians of
Lake Urumia, and many Jews, to this day. The Hebrew
speedily amalgamated with the old population of
Canaan, which contained enough Alpine (Hittite?)
blood to impart to many modern Jews a high-round

head and a large nose. Somewhere in their history
the Jews acquired a Finno-Ugrian or Mongolian tinge
that crops out occasionally in slightly almond eyes.
In Africa Semites share the physical characteristics
of their Hamitic-speaking neighbours, being more or
less beardless, woolly-haired, and dark-skinned. Even
the Arabs, in the old Semitic home-land, have not
escaped contamination. In the south they have the
small calf that is found among many Hamites, and often
Negro blood.

If we take modern Arabs of Najd as the purest
surviving specimens of the old Semitic type, we may say
that it resembled the Mediterranean, and lacked the
Negroid suggestions of most Hamitic peoples.

Cultural Types

As the original Semites were racially influenced,
so they were also culturally shaped, by their different
environments. They took up the occupations of
people whom they found, and they were obliged to meet
the inexorable conditions of struggle for survival in the
places to which they had committed themselves.
Phoenicians found themselves with backs to the mountains and faces to the sea. Their experiments in navi-
gation and trade proved successful, and they were
gradually shaped by selection into a sea-faring people,
very different from their sheep-tending ancestors of the
desert. In another environment perhaps Israel would
have produced great architecture and sculpture, or
great philosophy, instead of the Law and the Prophets.

Most of the common generalisations about Semites
are applicable to certain Semitic peoples only. The
Yahweh religion was, with difficulty and indifferent
success, imposed upon the Hebrews by one of their
tribes. Later, and in a different form, it was very
successfully forced upon the Arabs by a single man.
Monotheism is not likely to have been the religion of
primitive Semites, nor were most Semitic nations
monotheistic.

ABYSSINIAN SEMITE.
Native of Tigrè, northern Abyssinia, of Semitic speech and
of Semitic-Hamitic stock with a Negro strain.

AKKADIANS AND SUMERIANS

When the curtain of history rises upon Babylonia it is still called the Land of Shinar. In the South of it are settled the Sumerians; along their northern border the Akkadians. The Sumerians had come into Shinar from the mountains to the east, bringing with them their air-god, En-Lil, for whom they had to construct an artificial mountain at Nippur. The Akkadians had come from the Arabian desert: not directly, via the Wādi ar-Rumma, but from the north, down along the course of the Euphrates. They had left behind them on the Tigris, a colony of kinsmen who were more remote from Sumerian influence, and presumably of purer Semitic stock. The Sumerians were of Mongolian or Mongoloid (Finno-Ugrian?) origin. The Akkadians were Semites. The Sumerians spoke an agglutinative language, with vowel-harmony and no gender; and wrote in a system of conventionalised pictures, shaped by their type of speech into syllable-signs, exactly like Chinese. The Akkadians spoke an inflected language, having tri-consonantal roots, vowel-gradation, and gender, and had no writing. The Sumerians worshipped the elements, particularly the god of the air, as the modern Chinese peasant is prone to do. The Akkadians probably worshipped spirits who lived in places which they frequented, and a spirit which followed their tribe as it wandered about. Altogether, the two races were as different as they could possibly be.

AMALGAMATION

By about 2700 B.C. the Akkadians had conquered all Shinar, and the entire Fertile Crescent, from Persia to the Mediterranean. Within a few centuries they had completely blended with the Sumerians, although the old division of the land into Sumer and Akkad persisted. The Semitic tongue of the Akkadians prevailed as the national language, while the old Sumerian language continued, as the "Latin" of religion and letters, down almost to the beginning of the Christian Era. The Sumerian system of writing was pressed into service for writing Akkadian. This was unfortunate, for Akkadian was a language of fixed consonantal roots and significantly changing vowels, requiring an alphabet of consonants, including some very peculiar ones; whereas the Sumerian writing consisted of signs for fixed syllables, and only such ones as were convenient to the agglutinative Sumerian language. In this way Akkadian was so distorted that vital distinctions, such as difference in the length ("doubling") of consonants appear to have been lost. It is not unlikely, however, that the actual pronunciation of Akkadian was gradually modified under the influence of the alien Sumerian. This probably took place through Sumerian mothers and nurses.

LATER SEMITIC INFUSIONS

Just before 2200 B.C. a Semitic people of Palestine and Syria, the Amorites, took possession of Shinar, making the obscure town of Babylon its capital. These people were themselves not pure Semites, of course, but mixed with unknown elements from the west. Very much later, at about 1400 B.C., the Semitic Aramaean hordes inundated the border-lands of the Syrian Desert, so that Aramaic became the speech of Babylonia in the days of the Jewish Exile, and continued to be such till the Arab conquests. They must have left physical effects upon the population.

CIVILISATION OF BABYLONIANS

The civilisation of the Babylonians cannot be considered apart from that of the Sumerians. In fact, when the Sumerian culture has been described, there remains very little to be said of the Semitic Babylonians. Their chief contributions were the Semitic deities of the sun and of the moon, their own peculiar god Marduk, and the great Asiatic love-goddess Ishtar.

Babylonian civilisation strikes us as distinctly inferior to Egyptian. Living in a land of clay, their architecture was from beginning to end heavily conditioned by the want of suitable building stone. Their sculpture is unlovely as a whole, the only exception being certain animal-portraits by the Assyrians. As lapidaries they excelled.

The most serious criticism of their culture is its materialism. Their religion concerned itself with two things: (1) Economic welfare, (2) immunity from devils. The temple-priesthood superintended agriculture and supported itself by its control of irrigation. The temple-cult did all things necessary in astrology, divination and exorcism, to protect the physical health of the people. The dead were buried without grace or imagination, usually in rough jars, under their dwellings. The Babylonians had only vague and depressing ideas about a future state, in which the good and the bad were indistinguishable. With them originated the merciless tradition of an "eye for an eye." They gave us the commercial unit of weight which we call the "pound," the sixty-minute hour, and the circle of six-times-sixty degrees. But the Egyptians left us evidence of a sense of beauty which glorified all that they touched, from their commonest utensils to their loftiest temples, and from village ethics to visions of immortality.

ASSYRIANS

On the upper Tigris there was building-stone. The climate was cooler and more bracing than that of the Babylonian plains. There was little or no Sumerian blood in the veins of the Assyrian. He shared the Sumerian-Akkadian civilisation of his southern cousins, but he was in contact with the Hittite culture of Asia Minor. The Akkadian system of writing he enlarged and improved. The old Akkadian literature he collected, copied, and zealously preserved. Under the inspiration of the old Babylonian lapidary's art he

carved beautiful figures of animals on alabaster slabs.
But the Assyrian state is without a parallel in history
for economic destructiveness, organised rapacity, and
calculated frightfulness. The cruelty of the Assyrian
is a thing that stands out hideously, even in a part of
the world where inhumanity is common. His greater
energy and efficiency he devoted effectively to war.
He fought with chariots and horses, with the new iron
weapons of the Hittites, and with battering-rams of his
own invention. Like the Sumerian and Babylonian,
he looked forward to no future state of reward or
punishment. His chief god was the war-god Asshur.
He set the example of world empire, followed in turn by
the Persians, Greeks, Romans, French, and Prussians.
He made no other contributions to civilisation.

CHALDAEANS

The Chaldaean phase of Babylonian civilisation
resulted from an internal movement, and did not involve
any racially different group of peeple. The Neo-
Babylonian Empire represented a brief renaissance of
old Babylonian glory after the extinction of Assyria
and before the rise of Persia. It is important because
it is the Babylon of the Exile. But it was an age that
busied itself with the past.

THE AKKADIAN LANGUAGE

The written language of Babylonia and Assyria was
in all periods essentially the same. The forms of
cuneiform writing, however, underwent modification
in the course of time and in different localities. Four
periods of the language are distinguished: (1) Old Akkadian, at about 3000, and again at about 2250 B.C.
(2) Middle Akkadian, occasional Babylonian and
Assyrian, toward the end only Assyrian sources of
about 1100 B.C. (3) Neo-Akkadian, almost exclusively
Assyrian sources, from 850 to 606 B.C. (4) Late
Akkadian, the archaic and artificial written language

of the Neo-Babylonian empire. During all this time
the vernacular was going its own way, as business
documents show. In the last period Aramaic was
becoming the every-day language of Babylonia.

SUMERIAN SOUNDS

The old Sumerian language possessed the vowels
a, e, i, u, and the consonants:

	Labials.	*Dentals.*	*Velars.*
Stops	b	d	g
	p	t	k
Fricatives		z	g̣
		s ʃ	
Vibrants		r	
Nasals	m	n	
Laterals		l	

Like South German and Turkish, Sumerian did not
distinguish sharply between the voiced and voiceless
stops, so that **b, d, g** were confused with **p, t, k.**

AKKADIAN SOUNDS

The Semitic Akkadians began to write their language
in the Sumerian syllabary, which permitted the representation of no more than the above, very limited, stock
of consonantal sounds. They found means of representing the additional sounds **ṭ,**[52] **ṣ, x, q, ʔ,** and must
therefore have felt the necessity of distinguishing them.
Four of these are Semitic sounds, and three of them are
"emphatics."[52]

They did not see fit to find signs for **h, ḫ, ʕ,** and did
not use the signs for **g̣, j (i),** which Sumerian already had,
but wrote **ʔ** in place of **j, g̣, h, ḫ, ʕ.** These five sounds
must therefore have been wanting in Akkadian.

Sumerian influence was so strong among Babylonians (as contracted with Assyrians) that they often

---

[52] Of what sort? Perhaps, e.g., tˀʕ or tš.

confused the voiced and voiceless stops, in the manner
of Sumerian, failed to distinguish the "emphatics,"[52]
and otherwise displayed a dull and foreign ear, and a
heavy and alien tongue. The usual confusions are
between:

    (1) **b** and **p**
    (2) **d, t,** and **ṭ**[52]
    (3) **g, k,** and **q**
    (4) **z, s, ʃ, ṣ, l,** and **r**
    (5) **w, m,** and **n.**

The disregard of length, whether of vowel or consonant, is a striking non-Semitic peculiarity which is
seen also in Turkish and Armenian. But, as it is also
found in Russian and Spanish, nothing can be made
of the fact.

A complete list of the Akkadian and Assyrian consonants would be:

	Labials.	*Dentals.*	*Velars.*	*Uvulars.*	*Laryngals.*
Stops	b	d	g		
	p	t ṭ[52]	k	q	?
Fricatives	w	z			
		s ʃ ṣ	x		
Vibrants		r			
Nasals	m	n			
Laterals		l			

THE NAME "CANAANITE"

The name "Canaanite" applies properly to the
inhabitants of the lowlands of Palestine. In a broader
sense it is made to include all the people of Palestine
and Syria who spoke the Canaanitish language: Moabites,
Ammonites, Edomites, "Canaanites" living in contact
with Israel, Phoenicians, and Amorites.

RACE

The Canaanites, as the people of Palestine, formed a
cultural and linguistic group. Politically they were

Photograph by]   [*Vester & Company, Jerusalem.*

DURZI (DRUSE).

The Durūz (Druses) are a religious sect of the Lebanon, in-bred since the tenth century A.D. Their religious exclusivism is probably the continuation of a racial one, which may be Canaanitish-Aramaean.

divided. Exactly what they were racially we have no means of knowing. Even at the beginning of our historical knowledge Palestine must have contained the deposit of many migrations, back and forth, between Asia and Africa; for Palestine lies upon one of the great highways of the nations. It is fairly safe to say that that deposit contained little or no Yellow or Black blood. One of its constituents was Alpine, another was perhaps Mediterranean, if the dolmens mean anything. Its chief ingredient was probably Semitic. It may have been very much modified from the Semitic type of the desert, but for all that fairly uniform within Palestine. The "Lip of Canaan" (Isaiah xix. 18) was the language of all Canaanites, whether in Palestine or in Syria, and the bond of unity between them. In the time of the Tell el-Amarna letters (c. 1375–1358 B.C.) we find an Egyptian governor writing to the Pharaoh in Akkadian, and introducing Canaanitish words as occasional glosses. In the course of their prolonged conquest and settlement of Palestine the Hebrew tribes, who began to filter in at about that time, gave up their natural speech, some form of Aramaic, and adopted Canaanitish. In course of time they regarded it as "Hebrew," and imagined it to have been used by Moses. Tradition says nothing of this important change of speech. But it must be remembered that primitive peoples are used to many languages, learn them easily, and take them for granted, except in rare moments of reflection.

CIVILISATION

Babylonia had left its impress upon Palestine and all the ancient Near East; but especially upon Palestine, as we learn from the Tell el-Amarna letters. Akkadian had lingered on as the official language ever since the days of Sargon of Akkad, when Palestine was part of a Babylonian state reaching from the mountains of Elam (Persia) to the Mediterranean.

Of Canaanitish civilisation we know little apart from the religious elements which come to light in the Old Testament account of religious struggles. They were an agricultural people, with whom the invading Hebrews dwelt, and from whom they learned the arts and habits of settled life. Along with the pursuit of agriculture went the worship of **be'ālīm,** the local "genii," or nature-spirits, of the places which they cultivated. This was a habit brought from Arabia, where even now every spot has its unseen denizens, the "jinn" of our Arabian Nights Entertainments. Unconsciously the Hebrews adopted the cult of the **be'ālīm**; and the difficulty which this caused the exponents of the Yahweh religion is a well-known theme of Old Testament writers. But in the end the purer Semitic blood of the Hebrews included the less pure blood of the Canaanites. At any rate, the Canaanites disappeared, and, as they could not have been exterminated, must have been absorbed into one resulting people. The well-known habits of a peasant population, and the story of Ruth, tell us what happened. Purity of blood, like purity of worship, were ideals rather than accomplished facts. It is this connection between Canaanite and Hebrew which makes the Canaanite particularly interesting to us.

RELIGION

The religious ideas of the Canaanites are too well known to require much comment. Their religion was essentially a cult of local and inchoate gods, not individualised like the gods of pagan Greece and Rome. Every man was his own priest. Sacrifice of the first-fruits of the soil, and of flocks and herds, was a natural tribute to the "proprietor" or "lord" (**ba'al**) of the farm. When he was appeased all went well. So also the first-born of the family was sacrificed, to secure the god's favour and insure the fruitfulness of the wife and abundance of offspring. It was this which so shocked

the gentle Romans when they came to know the
Phoenicians of Carthage. Sacrifice of the first-born
did not cease till after the Exile, and is perpetuated
to this day in the Jewish custom of ransoming a child
by giving the rabbi a present for the poor. The powers
of reproduction were worshipped. Sex-rites existed,
with sacred prostitutes, both men and women. Religious
prostitution still existed in the time when Genesis
xxxviii. 15 was written (c. 650 B.C.). Excesses of this
kind were known in the times of Amos and Hosea
(Amos ii. 7; Hosea iv. 14).

Some of the be'ālim were absorbed by the religious
figure of Yahweh, others became evil spirits, others
survive to this day in the superstitious practices of the
modern "Arab" peasantry of Palestine.

PHOENICIANS

If we choose to regard Hebrews as Aramaeans, which
they originally were, and not as Canaanites, which they
came to be, there remain of historically important
Canaanites only the Phoenicians.

The Phoenicians believed that they came from eastern
Arabia or the vicinity of the Persian Gulf. They may
have been at the fore-front of the great Semitic migration of about 2500 B.C., and thus have been pushed
out of Palestine proper into the narrow coastal plain,
between the Lebanon mountains and the Mediterranean.
It is supposed that they were already in possession of
the harbours on the coast as early as 2500 B.C. In 1300
they prevented Assyria from reaching the sea. In the
Tell el-Amarna letters they are still vassals of Egypt,
and presumably without colonies in the west. They
offered no resistance to the Hebrew invasion when at
last Egyptian power decayed; but, on the other hand,
were not much affected by it. Hiram I, king of Tyre
from about 968–935 B.C., ruled over a prosperous people
with some experience in sea-trading. He was able to
help King Solomon in his building operations (1 Kings v.

5 ff.) and sea-faring adventures (1 Kings ix. 26 ff.). A little later, in the ninth and eighth centuries B.C., we hear of the Sidonian Phoenicians through Homer. At that time the Phoenicians were the great traders and artificers of the Near East. Sidon was the older settlement, and Tyre, with its colony of Carthage, the younger. For a while Carthage threatened to divert or permanently change the course of history in the Mediterranean.

CIVILISATION

The Phoenicians occupied the coastal plain of Syria, from Caesarea almost to Laodicea. For some reason they made no attempt to conquer the people of the Lebanon, at their backs, but took to the sea; and ultimately founded colonies in North Africa, Spain, Cyprus, Crete, Sicily, Sardinia, and Malta, and on the coasts of the Black Sea and the Ægean. They passed Gibraltar, and followed the coast of Europe as far as the Weichsel on the Baltic. They circumnagivated Africa. Possibly they even reached the Azores and Cornwall. They were undoubtedly among the world's first great navigators.

ALPHABET

It is unfortunate that Phoenicians, like other Canaanites, have left us no literature, and indeed seem to have had few books. Otherwise they might have given most interesting accounts of what their navigators and traders saw in their wanderings of that far-off age. In their manufactures they were unoriginal, imitating the designs of Egypt and Babylonia. But, as inventors of the alphabet, they are entitled to a high place in the history of culture.

Egypt had long before produced a perfect alphabet, but lacked the courage and enterprise to use it. After coming into contact with Babylonian culture the Persians invented an alphabet of cuneiform signs; but they soon went over to the use of the Aramaean language, and the Phoenician alphabet in which it was written. The origin of the Phoenician letters is still undecided. The presumption is that they arose out of some syllabic and ultimately ideographic system; but neither Egyptian nor Babylonian was the direct source. They may have been devised (in imitation of the Egyptian alphabet?) out of trade signs or brand-marks used by Mediterranean traders, as Petrie has suggested.[53] However that may be, they first appear at about 1000 B.C., spreading westward through the Greeks and Romans, and eastward through the Aramaeans, to become at last the alphabet of the greater part of the inhabited earth.

CANAANITISH LANGUAGE

Hebrew has been preserved in the writings of the Old Testament, Phoenician in a large number of inscriptions from many parts of the Mediterranean world, and Moabitish in a single monument of Mesha. Almost no old Hebrew inscriptions, and no Phoenician literature has survived. Of other Canaanites we have neither monumental nor literary remains.

Phoenician and Moabitish are so closely akin to Hebrew that all three may be called dialects of one language. The chief characteristic of the group is change of Semitic long **ā** into **ō** (as in Hebrew) or even **ū** (as in Punic). This tendency may be a heritage from earlier inhabitants of Phoenicia. It is perpetuated in certain Arabic dialects of Syria. The other characteristic is change of all so-called **th**-sounds (Ꝋ, **ð**, Ꝋ, **ḏ**) into corresponding **s**-sounds (ʃ, **z**, **ṣ**). This must have occurred by acoustic error, not by ordinary processes of sound change among a homogeneous people. It is paralleled by the Persian or Turkish pronunciation of Arabic, or a Frenchman's attempt to pronounce English: "the," "this"; and argues alien influence in ancient Canaan. In Homeric times, however, as we learn from

[53] *The Formation of the Alphabet*, 1912.

I

the Odyssey, ancient Semitic ǝ must still have been
heard, for **Tyros** begins with a **t** and not with an **s**-sound.
Phoenician is distinguished by a later vocabulary,
and the loss of that habit of using tenses with reversed
values which we have already noticed.[54] Moabitish,
so far as we know, differed only in having an extra
derived stem in its verb.

The Old Testament is a rather small collection of
writings, composed or redacted with a religious purpose,
and not completely representative of ancient Hebrew.
Its oldest parts date from about 1000 B.C.; but its
language, as now "punctuated" (vowelled) is no older
than the seventh century A.D. The late, liturgical
pronunciation represented by this text is certainly not
the pronunciation of living ancient Hebrew; but it is
nevertheless remarkably free from the influence of
Aramaic.   Post-biblical Hebrew is an artificial language
of the schools, of no use for the present inquiry.

There is some reason to believe that even the consonantal text of the Old Testament does not represent
all the sounds once found in Hebrew; for the Greek Old
Testament has "Gaza" spelled with a **g** where the
Hebrew text has ʿ.   The long vowels of old Hebrew
are generally represented by the consonants **h, w,** and **j.**
The secondary long vowels, and the short vowels, are
known only through the later pointing.   Jews from
different parts of the world read Hebrew differently,
and do this not entirely because of their different
vernaculars.

Sounds of Canaanitish

In its earliest stages Canaanitish seems to have had
all the Semitic sounds of Arabic, and in addition an old
north-Semitic **s**-sound, represented by שׂ and probably
equivalent to ç. Very early, and probably under
foreign influence, it changed all its **th**-sounds to **s**-sounds.
In a later stage the sounds **ḥ** and **x**, and ʿ and **ġ** coalesced.

[54] See p. 65.

In the latest stage, under very strong foreign influence, pressure-articulation was given up. But the history is a long one, and many dialectic differences must have existed in the same age.

In Hebrew a new phonetic peculiarity appeared; the sounds **b, g, d, k, p, t,** after a vowel became *β*, **g, ð, x, ɸ, ɵ**. This principle may have been shared by other Canaanitish dialects, or it may have been derived from Aramaic. In early Hebrew **ç** was similar to **ʃ**, but eventually became like **s**.

It would be difficult to construct a single table to represent Canaanitish sounds because of the many changes which the language underwent at different times and in different places.

ARAMAEANS

By the term "Aramaean" we mean all those peoples who came out of Arabia with the great Semitic migration of about 1500 B.C. Some of these peoples, like the Hebrews, adopted another language. On the other hand, the Aramaic language—or rather, group of dialects—came at times to be spoken by non-Aramaeans, such as the later Babylonians. Mesopotamia, as their chief settlement, was for a time called, after them, "Aram," and they in turn were later called, after it, "Syrians." "Aramaean" is therefore chiefly an ethnic name, although at times it is applied to peoples of not very pure Aramaean stock who spoke Aramaic or lived in Syria.

At about 1400 B.C. Aramaean nomads were attempting to take Syria and Palestine; by about 1300 they had done so; in Syria retaining their own speech, in Palestine discarding it for the older language of Canaan. By 1200 they were strong enough in Syria to prevent the Assyrians from reaching the Mediterranean coast; and thereafter produced a group of flourishing kingdoms in the west.

CIVILISATION

The Aramaean migration was a very large one. For some reason or other the Aramaic dialects were quickly and widely adopted. But of Aramaean civilisation there is little to be said. This is partly because their ancient cities have not been sufficiently studied; but chiefly because they adopted the older culture which they found, and left no deep imprint of their own upon it.

As the Phoenicians were great merchants on the sea, so the Aramaeans were great traffickers on the land; and from about 1000 B.C. onward they spread the Phoenician alphabet among all the peoples with whom they traded. Their manner of writing was so much more convenient than the cuneiform that it displaced the latter in Babylonia. With the writing went Aramaic speech, a simpler form of Semitic. In the end Aramaic became the language of people whose fathers had called themselves Babylonians and Assyrians. It was the official language of the Old Persian (Achaemenian) Empire, employed even in provinces where it was as little the natural speech of the governed as of the governors. It was the written language of the Arabic-speaking Nabataean kingdom, with its capital at Petra; and was used by Arabs even at Teima, within Arabia itself. It was the language of Palestine in the days of Jesus. The Gospel according to Mark is a thinly veiled Aramaic book; and some sixteen Aramaic words have survived even in our common English New Testament. Aramaic was the language of the mother church in Palestine down to the Arab conquest; and is still the sacred tongue of the Syrian (Jacobite) and Assyrian (Nestorian) churches. As the language of the Jews after the decay of Hebrew, it became the vehicle of their exegetical and theological literature in Targum and Talmud. It dominated the Pahlavi Persian of the Sasanian Empire. It still survives near Damascus and Mosul, and especially among the Nestorian Christians of north-west Persia. But, as there was no

Photograph by]   [*Vester & Company, Jerusalem.*

NUṢAIRI.

The Nusairiyah are a religious sect in the mountains of
northern Syria, originally from somewhere on the Euphrates,
in-bred since the tenth century A.D.   Their religious exclusivism is probably the continuation of a racial one,
which may be Aramaean.

Photograph by]   [*Vester & Company, Jerusalem.*

JEWISH TYPE.

This well-known Jewish type suggests no recent admixture, and may well be a survival from the days of the Prophets.

Photograph by]   [*Vester & Company, Jerusalem.*

MOORISH JEW.

The Sephardic or Spanish-Portuguese Jews of the Barbary
States are Spanish-Arab in culture and speech, and sometimes resemble physically the Berbers among whom they
live. Their pronunciation of Hebrew is very pure and
primitive, and they have been thought to be of Judaean
origin.

great Aramaean civilisation and no Aramaean nation, there could be no great Aramaic literature. Syriac, the language of the church of Edessa (Urfa) and of the Jacobite and Nestorian churches, is the best known Aramaic idiom. Its literature is voluminous, but disappointing in content.

HEBREWS AND JEWS

The Hebrews were roughly identical with the Khabiri of the Tell el-Amarna letters, who moved across the Jordan into Palestine between 1400 and 1200 B.C. as part of the great Aramaean migration. One group, becoming diverted through Sinai into the Delta of the Nile, was enslaved by the Pharaoh, and finally delivered from bondage by a great lawgiver, Moses. This group brought with it into southern Palestine the cult of Yahweh, a divinity associated with a certain sacred mountain in Sinai. The other Hebrew tribes crossed into Palestine from east of the Jordan and gradually conquered the older Semitic inhabitants. The majority, in the north, were rather easily assimilated; but the minority, in the south, living under hard conditions, in constant contact with the desert and its stern simplicity and democracy, and devoted to the worship of Yahweh, remained opposed to the Canaanitish culture with its luxury and licence. These southern or Judaean Hebrews thus remained much purer in blood than their northern brethren. Of the northern Hebrews the majority were deported and lost among the nations. The remainder were left upon the soil to mingle with the motley migration from Babylonia, and ultimately became the people of the Samaritans. The southern Hebrews were deported also, but returned from Babylon after scarcely fifty years, during which they suffered probably very little admixture of foreign blood. From the days of Ezra onward there was less chance than ever of admixture; for the Hebrew nation had become a Jewish Church, strictly endogamous, and not often given to proselytising.

When we examine modern Jews, from the Barbary States, from Yemen, from Persia, from Georgia, from China, from Abyssinia, and from eastern Europe, we find them surprisingly like the gentiles among whom they dwell.   It has been suggested that natural environment has exerted an influence upon them by its selective action; and that the social environment has exerted an influence also by dictating standards of beauty and desirability in mating.   Perhaps it must be admitted that races which are in contact are bound to mingle. This is particularly true where wars and persecutions often leave women the unwilling mothers of a hybrid offspring.   Even where there is peace, and where the strongest of tabus exist, as in the United States, the extremely alien Negro is being slowly absorbed.

ARAMAIC LANGUAGE

Aramaic, like Arabic, became a great international language.   But Aramaic spread by virtue of its simplicity, and the ubiquity of the traders who spoke it; whereas Arabic, a very primitive and difficult tongue, followed in the train of a conquering theocratic host and a divine Arabic Book, the Koran.

Why, of two languages fresh from the desert, one should be simple and the other complex, it is impossible to say.   Aramaic, of course, emerged directly from the northern Semitic centre, while Arabic came via the northern from the southern.   But there is no evidence of foreign contact, to justify such great decay as Aramaic has suffered at the very beginning of our knowledge of it.

The general decay shows itself in three ways: (1) Simplification of inflection, especially in the verb. (2) Simplification of sentence-structure, especially the use of participles and auxiliary verbs. (3) Weakening or loss of sounds involving the "pressure-articulation."

Photograph by]   [*Vester & Company, Jerusalem.*

YEMENITE JEW.

The Jews of Yemen resemble the southern Arabs with whom they have doubtless intermarried. Their pronunciation of Hebrew is, on the other hand, in certain respects like that of the Ashkenazic Jews of Europe. They settled at different times in South Arabia, but especially after 70 A.D. In the sixth century A.D. a certain Dhū Nuwās ("Man with the Side-Locks") induced all Yemen and Himyar to accept Judaism.

GERMANIC JEW.

The Ashkenazic or German Jews of eastern Europe are Slavic in culture and Germanic in speech, sometimes resembling in appearance the Finno-Ugrian-Nordic Slavs among whom they live. Their pronunciation of Hebrew is decidedly un-Semitic, and they have been thought to be of northern Hebrew origin. Most of them doubtless came from their settlements on the Rhine, at the time of the Crusades. Some of them may be descendants of Aryan-Ugrian Khazars who adopted Judaism in the middle of the eighth century A.D. About eleven-twelfths of the Jews of the world are Ashkenazic.

Photograph by]   *[Vester & Company, Jerusalem.*

SAMARITAN.

The Samaritans are northern Hebrews with a large admixture
of various non-Hebrew but mostly Semitic elements, in-bred.

SOUNDS OF ARAMAIC

There were so many varieties of Aramaic, and they tend to such unphonetic spelling, that it is difficult to speak of Aramaic sounds in general.

In its early stages Aramaic had, like Canaanitish, lost its old Semitic **th**-sounds, ϴ, ð, ϴ, ð̣. But, whereas Canaanitish had changed them to the corresponding **s**-sounds, ʃ, **z**, ṣ, Aramaic changed them to the corresponding **t**-sounds, **t**, **d**, ṭ. The Aramaic change is a natural one within a homogeneous community, as when the old Germanic **th**-sounds of English "thin," "this" become in German **d**ünn and **d**ies; but the Canaanitish change is one which argues foreign influence. This change in Aramaic therefore is presumably an old one, antedating its dispersion.

Another very early sound change is that which apparently converted ð̣ into ʕ or **q**. We see at once that the ancient sound could not have been ð̣, but must have been ðʕ or ðʔʕ, the old Hamitic and Abyssinian form of the pressure-articulation.[55] The principal articulation, ð, has been lost, and only the pressure-articulation remains. **q** is the result of extreme elevation of the larynx.

Aramaic has only one sign for ç and **s**, for ɡ and ʕ, and for ḥ and **x**. It had probably lost ç, ɡ, and ḥ.

The tendency to confusion between ʔ, ʕ, and **q** shows that ʕ was made with a complete closure, as in modern Syrian Arabic, and was therefore really ʔʕ.

Aramaic, like Hebrew changes the sounds **b, g, d, k, p, t,** after a vowel into β, ɡ, ð, **x**, φ, ϴ. This may be original with Aramaic and secondary with Hebrew. It is unknown in other Semitic languages, except the nigridised Amharic of Abyssinia.

THE ARABS

The name "Arab" is often applied to all the inhabitants of Arabia in every age; but in a narrower

---

[55] See p. 57.

sense it means the people of Arabia who speak or spoke dialects of North Arabic or South Arabic. Except for some obscure references, North Arabs do not appear upon the scene of history before the unfolding of Islamic power in the seventh century A.D., and therefore fall outside the limits of our study. But the South Arabs have something to do with the Old Testament and may engage our attention.

The oldest South Arabian power was Maʿān (Maʿīn), flourishing in the days of Saul and David, or at about 1000 B.C. with its base in the south-west corner of the peninsula and its trade route via Mecca, Medina, and Maʿān to the Mediterranean port of Gaza. The biblical writers[56] call it Maʿīn or Maʿōn.

It was succeeded in the seventh century B.C. by the kingdom of Sheba, or the Sabaeans, controlling about the same territory, and having as its northern vassals Midian, or the Midianites. For Israel the Sabaeans were a remote and almost legendary folk,[57] of proverbial wealth[58] because they exported articles of luxury to the western world. The mythical Queen of Sheba[59] belongs to this period, some three centuries after Solomon.

After Sheba and Midian we hear of Kedar and Nebaioth, wild tribes, belonging to the fourth Semitic migration, of about 500 B.C., who plundered Judah, Edom, Moab, and Ammon in the latter days of the Southern Kingdom and after its fall. They pushed the Edomites out of their old lands into southern Judah, and brought into the east-Jordan land the Arab stock which later appeared as the Nabataeans, with their capital at Petra. As part of this group the Old Testament mentions Shalem (which we wrongly read "Solomon"), and later the Nabataeans.[60]

The names of many kings of Maʿān are known, and to some extent their order of succession, but not their

[56] 1 Chron. iv. 41; 2 Chron. xx. 1 (Greek text); xxvi. 7; Judges x. 12.
[57] Joel iii. 8; Psa. lxxii. 10.   [58] Psa. lxxii. 15.   [59] 1 Kings x. 1–10.
[60] Song of Songs, i. 5; 1 Macc. v. 25.

Photograph by]   *[Vester & Company, Jerusalem.*

NORTH ARAB MAN.

NORTH ARAB WOMAN.

chronology. All the Nabataean kings are recorded, from the first, Aretus (Ḥārith) I (169 B.C.), to the last, Rabil II (70–95 A.D.).

THE ARABIC LANGUAGE

When supplemented by Ethiopic, Arabic is rightly regarded as the most typical and primitive of Semitic languages, and is constantly referred to in questions of Semitic morphology and lexicography. Certainly no other one language equals it as a basis for Semitic philological study; and it has the added advantages of an abundant literature, a native grammatical cultivation, and a living tradition.

On the other hand, Arabic belongs to a later phase of Semitic than Akkadian or Ethiopic; and its vocabulary is often younger than Hebrew or even Aramaic. It may be called "the Sanskrit of Semitic languages"; but it is far from being primitive Semitic.

ARABIC SOUNDS

Classical Arabic, as cultivated by the poets of Arabia in the seventh century A.D., appears to have had the following consonantal sounds:

	Labials.	Dentals.	Palatals.	Velars.	Uvulars.	Laryngals.
Stops	b	d dʒ				
		t ṭ		k	q	ʔ
Fricatives	w	ð z ẓ̌	j	ǥ		ʕ
	f	θ s θ̣ ṣ ʃ		x		h ḥ
Vibrants		r				
Nasals	m	n				
Laterals		l				

It will be seen that the **th**-sounds (θ, ð, θ̣, ð̣) have all been preserved, as well as the distinction between **ḥ** and **x** and **ʕ** and **ǥ.**

On the other hand, ç has become confused with s, p has become f, g has become dʒ, and the "emphatic" sounds have nothing left of the pressure-articulation but a u-resonance caused by the elevation of the larynx and base of the tongue.

South Arabic is known to us only in inscriptions. It had the sound ç and, to judge from Ethiopic, may have had an older form of the emphatics.

North Arabic, then, was very conservative, and South Arabic doubtless most conservative, in phonology, as indeed we should expect the Semitic of Arabia to be.

CHAPTER VII.

Aryans

The Aryan Migration

ARYAN-SPEAKING Nordic Whites up to about 3000 B.C. lived a nomadic life somewhere west of the Ural Mountains and north of the Black Sea, the Caucasus, and the Caspian. At this time probably a gradual desiccation of the Russian grass-lands and a gradual increase of population had brought about an economic crisis; and a series of dry seasons, or even historical events of which there is no record, overcame the inertia of the great nomadic community, and set it in motion, in every possible direction. They could not well move eastward; for here they encountered another, the Mongol, nomadic community in the same plight as themselves. Toward the west the path was open; and they flowed in successive waves over northern Europe, over central Europe, partly peopled by Alpines, and over western and southern Europe, inhabited by Mediterraneans. Toward the south their path was obstructed by three formidable obstacles: the Black Sea and the Caspian, and the intervening wall of the Caucasus. They could enter the Near East only via the Balkans and Asia Minor, or by going around the Caspian into Persia.

Aryans in the Near East

It was just after 2000 B.C. that Aryans began to appear in the Near East. After settling for a time in Persia and Turkestan (?), the branch which is called "Aryan" in a narrower sense separated into two groups, one, the Iranian, remaining in Persia, and the other, the Indian, making its way through the mountains into India, there to be modified in spite of itself by an unidentified race, the Dravidians. At about the same time the Aryan barons of Mitanni established themselves in Armenia. By the middle of the eighteenth century the Aryan dynasty of the Kassites had taken possession of Babylonia. In Asia Minor Aryans had conquered Alpine Whites of Caucasic speech and founded the Hittite power. Between 2000 and 1000 B.C. Hellenic tribes took possession of the Ægean world displacing and absorbing an earlier White Mediterranean race and civilisation in Crete and in Greece, and colonising the shores of Asia Minor. The Mycenaean culture of Greece does not concern us here. But Minoans, fleeing before the Hellenic invasion, settled on the southern part of the Canaanitish coast just as the Hebrews were invading the land. They still were called "Cretans" (**Kerētim**), but generally "Philistines"; and from their ethnic name has come the geographical "Palestine." On the shores of Asia Minor the Hellenes were opposed by an older people, allies of the Hittities, such as the Dardani, who were attacked by the Greeks in the Trojan War, in 1184 (?) B.C.

HITTITES

The Hittites were a composite people and a political confederacy. As a people they founded a capital at Khati (Bogaz Koei) and spread westward through Asia Minor as far as the sea. After about 1200 B.C. they extended their influence into Syria, where the weight of their empire lay until its extinction in the eighth century B.C.

Hittitie records are no earlier than the fifteenth century B.C. The language in which they are written, is plainly Aryan, but it is not the language which the records themselves call "Hittite." We must conclude then that the ruling caste used Aryan, and that the mass of the people spoke a different, if not a non-Aryan, language. The monuments of Egypt show two distinct types of faces in their portraits of Hittite prisoners.

No doubt the body of the Hittite people was Alpine White; and their language may well have been Caucasic, or akin to one of the extinct languages of Asia Minor. No one has yet been able to read the Hittite inscriptions written in Hittite characters. But very recently the clay tablets which Winckler and Puchstein found at Bogaz Koei in 1906–7 have been satisfactorily deciphered and explained by Witzel.[61] At first they seemed to contain a jargon of Akkadian and something else. Gradually it appeared that the Hittities used whole words and phrases of Akkadian and Sumerian, in the manner of an ideogram, and appended their own inflectional ending, to indicate how the word was to be pronounced in Aryan. As an illustration from English: **Xmas** = "Christmas," because **X** is the Greek letter **ch,** and stands for **Christos,** and **mas** tells how the symbol is to be rendered in the vernacular. Similarly one might write **ETCorth** = "and so forth," or **EGple** = "for example." This is a strange manner of writing, but it has parallels elsewhere. The Akkadians did the same thing with Sumerian; and the Sasanian Persians took Aramaic roots bodily and supplied them with Persian endings, pronouncing the whole as a pure Persian word.

Hittite has not been exactly placed within the Indo-European family. A few examples from Witzel's book will show how much it resembles other Aryan languages.

NOUNS

| | *Personal.* | | | *Impersonal.* |
	Sg.	Pl.	Sg.	Pl.
Nom.	-aš, -iš, -uš	-eš	–	-a (or long final vowel)
Gen.	-aš	-aš	-aš	-aš
Dat.	-i	-aš	-i	-aš
Acc.	-an, -in, -un	-uš	–	-a (or long final vowel)
Abl.	-az	-az	-az	-az
Inst.	-it	-it	-it	-it
Loc.	-i	-aš	-i	-aš

[61] See note 19.

POSSESSIVE PRONOUN
Singular.

	1.*p.*	2.*p.*	3.*p.*
Nom.	-miš	-tiš	-šiš
Gen.	-maš	-taš	-šaš
Dat.	-mi	-ti	-ši
Acc.	-min	-tin	-šin

VERB
Present.

	Sg.			Pl.	
1.*p.*	2.*p.*	3.*p.*	1.*p.*	2.*p.*	3.*p.*
-mi	-ši	-zi	-ueni	-teni	-anzi

VOWEL GRADATION
"That one."

Pointing forward.	Pointing backward.	Far away.
eniš	uniš	anniš

IRAN AND TURAN

Aryan-speaking Nordic nomads roamed the steppes of Russia, and Turanian-speaking Mongol nomads ranged over the grass-lands of western Siberia, with the Ural mountains between them as a natural barrier. From remote times the two were in contact. In the Finno-Ugrians they have blended racially and linguistically. Both races have repeatedly invaded the Near East by way of Persia; and the Persian people and their language must have been influenced by the contact, in spite of the eternal difference which the Persian makes between "Iran" and "Turan." Often, no doubt, invading hordes consisted of loose confederacies of Iranians and Turanians, as in the case of the Cimmerians, Scythians, and Parthians. This has given much trouble to scholars.[62] The Scythians appear now as Russian, now as Mongolian nomads. There are "White" and

---

[62] Cf. Neumann, *Die Hellenen im Skythenlande*, 1855, and *Hippocrates, De Aere*, 24 ff., with Mullendorf, in *Monatsberichte der Berliner Akademie*, 1866.

"Black" Khazars. Even of the Muscovite we say: "Scratch a Russian, catch a Tartar."

CIMMERIANS AND SCYTHIANS

Sargon, king of Assyria from 722 to 705 B.C., by destroying the Kingdom of Urartu (Ararat) on Lake Van foolishly removed his only protection against the Cimmerian hordes in Armenia and on the Black Sea coast. The Assyrians allied themselves accordingly with the Scythians, a people whom they call "Ashkuza," the Hebrew "Ashkenaz." According to Herodotus the Scythians drove the Cimmerians into Asia Minor and ruled in their place. They assisted the Assyrians against the Medes and the Chaldaeans. At the fall of Nineveh, 607 B.C., they turned, in their defeat, toward Palestine, and even attempted to attack Egypt.

THE MEDES

In the ninth century B.C. Iranian nomads appeared in Anzan, the later Media. Their capital, Ecbatana (Hagmatana, Hamadān) is mentioned by Tiglath Pileser (c. 1100 B.C.) as subject territory: but apparently this was only a boast. After repeated allusions to them in Assyrian inscriptions of the eighth and seventh centuries, and a reference in 2 Kings xvii. 6, we hear that a certain Medic chieftain, Phraortes (Fravartish), in 647 B.C. united Medic and Persian tribes, after some sort of revolt against Assyria. In 614 Cyaxares (Huvakhsha-tara) the Mede unsuccessfully attacked Nineveh, and in 612 took it with the help of Nebopolassar. He was succeeded by his son, Astyages, in 585 (?), who was overthrown by the Persian, Cyrus (Kurush) in 550. Henceforth the seat of power shifted from north-western to south-western Persia.

The Medes left behind them no literature and no inscriptions. Nothing is known of their language, unless the words of Zoroaster in the Gathas, the oldest parts of the Avesta, are in his own Medic dialect.

The Persians

"Pars" is the province on the eastern side of the
Persian Gulf from which both the Achaemenian and
Sasanian dynasties came, and from which Persia takes
its name. At about 630 B.C. the people of Pars moved
out of their province and founded the kingdom of
Anshan in what was ancient Elam. As we have seen,
Cyrus, King of Anshan, (559–529 B.C.) in 550 took
possession of Media. Though opposed by a con-
federary of Babylon, Egypt, Lydia, and Sparta, Cyrus
in 546 possessed himself of Sardis, the Lydian capital,
and by 540 became master of all the East. Babylon
fell into his hands easily in the following year, under
rather extraordinary circumstances.

Fall of Babylon

The Babylonian government at this time was in the
hands of the Chaldaeans, an alien military caste which
had offended the priesthood by its centralisation of
religion in the capital city. In the conflict which had
developed between the Medes and the Persians, the
Chaldaeans sided with their recent allies the Medes,
which caused the priestly party to side with the Persians.
The Jews who had been deported from Palestine by the
Chaldaeans naturally sympathised with the Persians.

The stress and strain between the two parties in
Babylon led to the enthronement of Nabonidus
(Nabuna'id) as a compromise. But Nabonidus, being
a Babylonian, favoured too much the priestly party;
and was quietly imprisoned, and replaced by his son,
Belshazzar (Belsharuṣur).

In the end Belshazzar was betrayed into the hands of
the Persians. That both the priestly party and the
Jews were in a measure responsible for this may be
inferred from the manner in which Cyrus treated them
both. He showed the utmost consideration for Nabonidus, and Babylonian civilisation and institutions,
particularly religion; and the exiled Jews he immediately

restored to Jerusalem, becoming thereby a Jewish national hero for all time.

The religious toleration of Cyrus is puzzling. Perhaps the circumstances under which he obtained Babylon taught him the value of conciliation. At any rate, he managed to appear to the Babylonian priesthood a worshipper of Marduk (Bel), and to the Jews a servant of Jehovah, while remaining a good Zoroastrian: "Thus saith Jehovah to His Messiah, to Cyrus. . . . I have surnamed thee though thou hast not known me. . . . I am Jehovah and there is none else. I form the Light and create Darkness."[63] His example was imitated by Alexander the Great at Siwa, in Egypt, and by the German Kaiser at the tomb of Saladin in Syria. Perhaps his repatriation of the Jews was only part of a general policy of restoration of captured gods and peoples, in reversal of the old policy of Babylonia and Assyria, somewhat influenced by a wise desire to eliminate from his capital the disaffected elements which had once betrayed it. However that may be, Persia has throughout its history frequently shown itself friendly to the Jews.

THE ACHAEMENIAN EMPIRE

The Old Persian Empire, which is the Persia of the Old Testament and of Greek and Latin authors, lasted from 550 to 330 B.C. Under Cambyses (Kambujya, 530–522) it included all of Persia and Media, Babylonia and Assyria, Mesopotamia, Armenia and Asia Minor, Syria and Palestine, Egypt and Libya. Darius (Darayavush, 521–485) organised satrapies and built imperial roads. Crossing the Bosphorus in 514 B.C., he took Thrace and Macedonia. The great expedition of Xerxes I (Khshayarsha, 485–465) failed, the cities of Asia Minor and the Greek islands, which his two predecessors had taken, were lost, together with Thrace and Macedonia. It was Alexander the Macedonian who put an end to the Persian Empire in 330 B.C.

[63] Isaiah xlv. 1 ff. The last words allude to the Persian dualism.

K

The Sasanian Empire

From 330 B.C. to 226 A.D., more than five hundred years, the Persian people were under alien rule and influence. Hardly had Hellenism begun to affect them when they were isolated from the West and subjected to the half-Turanian domination of the Parthians. It was during this time that the ancient Persian language, once as elaborate as Sanskrit, became Pahlavi ("Parthian"), practically the same as modern Persian in its extreme simplicity. This is a striking example of the effect on language of cultural upset and racial admixture.

After the Parthian domination the Persian people again asserted themselves and strove to revive the ancient glories of Iran in the Sasanian Empire. It lasted from 226 till 651 or 652 A.D., more than four hundred years, but it was only the shadow of the Old Persian Empire. The people had changed quite as much as their language. Manners and customs remind one of the Turks. They were no longer Aryans from the steppes, but Iranian-Turanian hybrids.

Islamic Persia

The Arab invasion put an end to the Sasanian Empire in 651 or 652 A.D., and gave the national life and language a new direction. The ancient religion was swept away. There was little left of Persian grammar to be shaken by this new collision; but the language lost a great part of its vocabulary to Arabic. The Arab racial and cultural infusion, however, was not bad; and Persia again was able to contribute to the world's stock of ideas. Look over the list of greatest names in Arabic literature and you will find that most of them are Persian.

In 1258 came the Mongol incursions, and later the Turkish invasions. If Europe suffered from these when nearly spent, what must have been their effect upon life and civilisation in Persia? It was here that

ARYANS

9

Turks and Mongols became Muslims, and took over a
great stock of Persian and Arab-Persian ideas and forms
of speech. As Persian was filled with Arabic, so Turkish
and Hindustani became filled with Persian.

PERSIAN CHARACTER

The strength, mildness, and wisdom of Cyrus and the
Old Persian regime contrast pleasingly with the short-
sighted cruelty and destructiveness of the Assyrians.
With great constructive insight the Persians restored,
placated, and compromised, dividing the Empire into
satrapies and uniting it by roads and post-routes, leaving
men as far as possible undisturbed in their ways of life,
even to the extent of making Aramaic the official
language of the state. Altogether the early Iranians
appear to have been a gifted race, capable of any
accomplishment.

But even under Darius began the decadence which is
associated with the Persian name. The cultural world
which they invaded with their vigorous hosts was
poisonous with the effluvia of rotting Babylon. The
land of Persia again and again was made to bear the
brunt of terrible Mongol and Turkish invasion. Mendacity, addiction to vice, and refined cruelty, became
their proverbial characteristics. Persian cruelty, as
we read of it in the story of the martyrs of Kharka or
in Morier's *Hajji Baba*, has a peculiar flavour, quite
unlike anything, except perhaps the Turkish. Its
outstanding quality is lack of imagination. That is
the precise difference to this day between Turks and
Arabs. The Persian mendacity is famous from the
days when Herodotus was assured that every Persian
youth was especially instructed to tell the truth.
Therein lies the great secret: Why should honest folk
be taught to tell the truth? Whether or not the
Persian has any conscience, apart from religious emotion,
it is certain that he has a great deal of the latter, and has
employed it in the service of ethics, or as a substitute

for character and good works. In the course of his
struggles with himself he has produced a number of
religious systems which are his chief contribution to the
world's stock of ideas.

ZOROASTRIANISM

In the seventh century B.C. Zoroaster (Zarathustra)
taught that Ahuramazda, the god of Good, whose
symbol was fire, waged eternal warfare with Ahriman,
the god of Evil, for the soul of Man whom Ahuramazda
had created. In this conflict Man might choose to help
or hinder, though the outcome was assured for the Good.
After death the souls of men were to be judged by
Ahuramazda according to their deeds in life, and reward
and punishment were to be meted out.

Here was a virile and hopeful faith, springing from a
rational and benevolent contemplation of life, and
actuated by a desire to do that which is Right. It was
immensely above and beyond the Sumerian and Akkadian
demonology and magic, or the Assyrian alliance of
Assur with his cruel hosts, or the Canaanitish rites of
sex and human sacrifice, or even the passive idealism
of the Osiris cult.

Zoroaster's discovery was the fundamental dualism
that underlies human experience. Do we not know
light and darkness, heat and cold, summer and winter,
birth and death, youth and age, growth and decay,
joy and sorrow? And is not life alternately glorified
by Good and corrupted by Evil?

The Semitic nomads of Arabia fear nature-spirits and
believe in manifestations of the dead; and this was
doubtless the philosophy of ancient Israel in spite of the
religion of Jehovah. But it is not Semitic to fear evil
spirits or postulate a great Evil Spirit. The demons
(šēdīm) of later Judaism are of Sumerian and Akkadian
origin, and Ashmedai is Persian.

Christianity, sprouting from Judaism when Persian
influence was strong, taught that God, though He could

end the conflict whenever He wished, yet permitted the great Adversary for a time to have his way with the souls of men, particularly if they chose to let him. It was hard to explain evil in a world entirely governed by an omnipotent and benevolent Diety.

MITHRAISM

In the Avesta and in the Vedas Mithra is a minor divinity having the same qualities as Ahuramazda. He is a god of Light and Truth. As time went on he became the patron of loyalty and the god of success, a mediator between man and inaccessible godhead, a redeemer of souls. Toward the end of the second century A.D. Mithraism had spread considerably among Roman soldiers, merchants, and slaves who were largely Asiatics. It was a good religion for the hopeless and all who daily faced hazards and uncertainties. It was a good religion for the Empire, because it taught obedience and the divine right of kings. Until definitely displaced in the fourth century A.D. it threatened to become the religion of the West.

MANICHAEISM

In the third century A.D. Mani taught that the universe arose out of an unfortunate mixture of Darkness and Light, and therefore was fundamentally bad. Salvation could come only at the end of the world, when Light would at last be released from its association with Darkness. Meanwhile nothing could be done about it.

Zoroastrians at this time were prepared to fight for Good and for the Persian religion. They despised the quietism and cosmopolitanism of Mani, and persecuted his followers. Christians were no less harsh with them. Muslims had no mercy upon them, even at times when the greatest consideration was shown to other faiths, as under the Abbasid Caliphs of Baghdad; for Manichaean dualism was offensive to Muslim monotheism. Mani's followers attempted to reconcile Zoroastrianism and Christianity. But these irreconcilables accused them of promiscuity; and Islam, the Religion of Submission, rooted them out for ever. Only in Europe, as the Albigenses, did they survive till the thirteenth century.

MAZDAKISM

In the sixth century A.D. Mazdak taught that all evils were due to the demons of Envy, Wrath, and Greed, which had destroyed the equality of mankind, decreed and desired of God; and that this equality must be restored. His followers were religious socialists and vegetarians, but they were branded as communists and libertines.

THE SHIITE CONSPIRACY

In the ninth century A.D. a Persian oculist, Maimun of Jerusalem, plotted a conspiracy against Islam and Arab rule which, carried out by several generations of his family and countless agents, honeycombed Muslim society with secret organisations and lodges, and confused it with esoteric doctrines, until a complete rupture between Persian and Arab was effected, and Islam was given a pantheistic and mystical direction in Persia which amounted to a different religion.

MODERN TIMES

In modern times, when the Persian people have sunk to a place of complete negligibility in the world's affairs generally, we observe the rise of Babism (in 1843), and its offshoot, Behaism (1863), with a vigorous following in the New World.

THE AREA OF REVEALED RELIGIONS

The "revealed" religions, each of which claims the unqualified support of all mankind, are sprung from a small area of the globe comprising Persia, India,

Palestine, and Arabia. Within this area men take an intuitive and emotional attitude toward experience, and believe that this subjective and personal attitude has the Divine sanction and a just claim to universal application. The faiths of Persia have failed; but a great part of the world lives by the teaching of Buddha, or Christ, or Muhammad. With honours equally divided between the "Aryans" and "Semites" of the Near East, shall we say that the secret is climatic or geographical?

Index

Lebanon, 17
Leontes, 18
Libya, 26, 127
Libyan Desert, 9
  plateau, 7
Libyan-Hamitic language, 54
Libyans, the, 8f., 45, 80 ff.
  names applied to, 48 f.
  supposed color of, 48 f.
Ligurian language, the 42

MA'ĀN, ("Magan"), 14, 118
Malaysia, 2
Manichaeism, 131
Marduk, 102, 127
Ma'rib, 14
Marriage of brother and sister, 89
Materialism, Babylonian, 103
Mazdakism, 132
Mecca, 12
Medes, 125 f.
Medinah, 12
Mediterranean race, the, 42 ff., 80 f., 87
Megaliths, 89 f.
Melanesians, 30
Memphis, 7
Mesha, monument of, 111
Mesopotamia, 3, 6, 19 f., 113
Midianites, 118
Migrations, Aramaean, 13
  Aryan, 121
  Canaanitish, 56
  causes of, 5
  Hamitic, 80
  into Fertile Crescent, 99
  nuclei of, 2
  Semitic, 5, 98,
  Turanian, 21
Minaean language, 66
Minaeans, the, 66
Mitanni, barons of, 122
Mithraism, 131
Moabites, the, 45
Moabitish language, the, 111
Mongol invasions, 128 f.
Mongolian traits, in Jews, 44
  in Sumerians, 45
Mongoloids, 87
Monosyllabic languages, 34, 35
Morphology, 39
Mosaic Dispensation, 10
Moses, 107, 115
Mountains, of Abyssinia, 8
  of Armenia, 2, 6
  of Asia Minor, 6

Caucasus, 21, 44, 121
  of Kurdistan, 6
mummification, 89

NABATAEANS, 98 f., 118 f.
Najd, 7, 12 f., 100
Natron Valley, 9
Neanderthal man, 30
Near East, ancient geography of, 1 ff.
  Aryans in, 121
  climate, ancient and modern, 2, 6
  drying out of, 3
  races of, 45
Nebaioth, 118
Nebopolassar, 125
Negro race, in Africa, 79 f.
  in Egypt, 83, 87
  in United States, 25, 28, 116
Negro (Sudanian) languages, character of, 55
Negroid Hamites, 54, 100
Neit, 83
Neolithic times, 1
Nestorian Christians, 99
  language of, 114
New Testament, 114
Nile River, 7
  people of valley of, 81
Nimrod, 24
Nineveh, 125
Nomads, 13, 16, 121
Nordic, 42 ff.
North Semitic languages, 95 ff.
Nubia, 90
Numerals, 56
Nursery words, 69
Nusairiyah, 114

OASES, Arabian, 9
  Libyan, 9
Oman, 11, 13
Organic structure in language, 35
Orontes, 18
Osiris, legend of, 83, 89

PAHLAVI (Middle Persian), 40
Palestine, 1, 6
  early geopraphy of, 17
  early inhabitants of, 19
  immigrants to, 19, 98, 107, 113
  language of, 114
Palmyra, 3

Papuans, 29
Parthians, the, 44 f., 124, 128
Persia, geography of, 20
  language of, 38, 123 f., 128
  people of, 44, 121, 129
  under Islam, 128
Persian Empires, 126 ff.
Persian Gulf, the, 2, 6 f., 19, 109
Petra, 3, 118
Pharaonic type, 80, 85
Phoenician language, the, 111
Phoenicians, the, 45, 99 f., 109 ff.
Phonetic symbols, table of, 41
Phraortes, 125
Plain of Esdraelon, 18
Poetry, Arabic, 16
Polarity, in Hamitic, 60
  in Semitic, 61
Polynesia, 2, 27
Pork-tabu, 89
Portraits, Hittite, 122
"Pressure-articulation," 57 f., 92, 116
Primitive man, life of, 31

RACE, anthropological account of, 29
Racial purity, in Arabia, 13
  of Hebrews, 108
Races, classification of, 24 ff.
  of Africa, 54 ff., 79 ff.
  of Europe, 42 ff.
Red Sea route, 15
Religion, Akkadian, 130
  area of revealed, 133
  Assyrian, 130
  Babylonian, 108
  Canaanitish, 108, 130
  Egyptian, 83 f., 88, 130
  Hebrew, 115
  Libyan, 83
  Persian, 130
Rivers of Palestine, 16
Roman soldiers and Mithraism, 131
Roots, Hamitic-Semitic, 47, 55, 67 f.
Ruba' al-Khāli, Desert of, 11
Russia, 5, 7, 121, 124

SABAEANS, the, 45, 118
Sahara Desert, the, 1 f., 54, 79
San'a, 12
Sasanian Empire, 128
Scandinavians, in Minnesota, 28
Scythians, the, 44 f., 124 f.

Semites, the, 23, 54 ff., 94 ff.
  early groups of, 13
  migrations of, 5, 7, 12, 19, 55 f., 98
  religion of, 130
Semitic nomads, 130
Semitic speech, 35 ff., 54 ff., 79, 94 ff .
  early, 12 f.
  Northern variety of, 95 ff.
Set, 83
Shalem, 118
Shatt al-Arab, 19
Sheba, Queen of, 118
Shem, 23
Shilh, 80
Shinar, 20, 101 f.
Sinai, Desert of, 1, 3, 10, 115
Sīwa, Oasis of, 9
Slavs, the, 44, 46
Social-reciprocal conjugation, 66
Somali speech, 76 f., 80, 85
South Arabia, 118
South Arabians, 99 f.
South Arabic, 94, 120
South Semitic languages, 95 ff.
  growth of, 33
  types, of, 34 ff.
Speech sounds as index of race, 38 f.
Stonehenge, 48
Strabo, 14
"Strandloopers," 31
Sudan, 79
Sudanic, 79
Suez, Gulf of, 10
Sumerian language, 101 f., 105, 123
Sumerians, the, 20, 44 f., 86, 101 f.
Sumero-Babylonians, the, 39
Syntax, index of race, 39
Syria, 1, 3, 6, 10, 96, 115
  fertility of, 18
  geography of, 98, 113
  harbours of, 18
  people of, 98, 113
Syriac, 96, 115
Syrian Desert, 16, 102

TALMUD, language of, 114
Taurus Mts., 22
Tell el-Amarna letters, 107, 109, 115
Ti, royal architect, 80
Tiglath Pileser, 125
Tigris and Euphrates, 7 f., 19, 87, 101
Time, Hamitic and Semitic expression of, 64

PRINTED BY
W. HEFFER & SONS LTD,
CAMBRIDGE, ENGLAND